MW00561786

AL

THE
iSRAELi
PROMETHEUS

VARDA YORAN
RINA SCHWIMMER

AL, THE ISRAELI PROMETHEUS

Copyright © 2018 Atlantic Publishing Group, Inc.

1405 SW 6th Avenue • Ocala, Florida 34471 • Phone 352-622-1825 • Fax 352-622-1875
Website: www.atlantic-pub.com • Email: sales@atlantic-pub.com
SAN Number: 268-1250

No part of this publication may be reproduced, stored in a retrieval system, or transmitted in any form or by any means, electronic, mechanical, photocopying, recording, scanning, or otherwise, except as permitted under Section 107 or 108 of the 1976 United States Copyright Act, without the prior written permission of the Publisher. Requests to the Publisher for permission should be sent to Atlantic Publishing Group, Inc., 1405 SW 6th Avenue, Ocala, Florida 34471.

Library of Congress Cataloging-in-Publication Data

Names: Yoran, Varda, author. | Schwimmer, Rina, author.
Title: Al, the Israeli Prometheus / by Varda Yoran, Rina Schwimmer.
Description: Ocala, Florida : Atlantic Publishing Group, Inc., [2018]
Identifiers: LCCN 2017059988 (print) | LCCN 2017060199 (ebook) | ISBN 9781620235263 (ebook) | ISBN 9781620235256 (pbk. : alk. paper) | ISBN 1620235250 (alk. paper)
Subjects: LCSH: Schwimmer, Al, 1917-2011. | Aerospace engineers—Israel—Biography. | Jews, American—Israel—Biography. | Aerospace industries—Israel—Officials and employees—Biography. | Israel-Arab War, 1948-1949—Participation, American. | Military aeronautics equipment industry—Israel—History—20th century.
Classification: LCC TL540.S366 (ebook) | LCC TL540.S366 Y67 2018 (print) | DDC 956.04/28 [B]—dc23
LC record available athttps://lccn.loc.gov/2017059988

LIMIT OF LIABILITY/DISCLAIMER OF WARRANTY: The publisher and the author make no representations or warranties with respect to the accuracy or completeness of the contents of this work and specifically disclaim all warranties, including without limitation warranties of fitness for a particular purpose. No warranty may be created or extended by sales or promotional materials. The advice and strategies contained herein may not be suitable for every situation. This work is sold with the understanding that the publisher is not engaged in rendering legal, accounting, or other professional services. If professional assistance is required, the services of a competent professional should be sought. Neither the publisher nor the author shall be liable for damages arising herefrom. The fact that an organization or Web site is referred to in this work as a citation and/or a potential source of further information does not mean that the author or the publisher endorses the information the organization or Web site may provide or recommendations it may make. Further, readers should be aware that Internet Web sites listed in this work may have changed or disappeared between when this work was written and when it is read.

TRADEMARK DISCLAIMER: All trademarks, trade names, or logos mentioned or used are the property of their respective owners and are used only to directly describe the products being provided. Every effort has been made to properly capitalize, punctuate, identify, and attribute trademarks and trade names to their respective owners, including the use of ® and ™ wherever possible and practical. Atlantic Publishing Group, Inc. is not a partner, affiliate, or licensee with the holders of said trademarks.

Printed in the United States

PROJECT MANAGER: Danielle Lieneman
INTERIOR LAYOUT AND JACKET DESIGN: Nicole Sturk

AL SCHWIMMER took tremendous risks to provide precious weapons and aerial defense secretly to the beleaguered Jews, outnumbered and threatened with extermination, who could not otherwise have withstood the attacks of five surrounding armies.

His was a crime, and he paid for it. His misdeeds created history. It turned the tide of Israel's war of independence and enabled the nascent nation to flourish.

This book was based entirely on the memoirs and memories as provided by Rina Schwimmer.

This book is dedicated to those whose skills, courage, ingenuity, passion, and commitment made it possible for the independence of the State of Israel to become a reality. In their hearts, they all know who they are.

I understood that doing what was right and doing what was lawful is not always the same.

I soon realized that to act morally, one must sometimes break the law.

Al Schwimmer

TABLE OF CONTENTS

1
GUILTY AS CHARGED

G U I L T Y ! screamed the headlines of all the major newspapers and the news correspondents across the airwaves on May 3, 1953. For over three years, the entire country had followed the drama unfolding in the courtroom. Guilty of one of the biggest military smuggling operations in American history, orchestrated by me, Al Schwimmer.

The Tinsel Town News in Los Angeles splashed mug shots of seven Americans indicted on September 30, 1949, accused of illegally sending military equipment of any kind to the Middle East in 1948. "Smugglers Transported Weapons, airplanes and parts stolen from US ordinance dumps," read their headlines.

"Schwimmer and Six Other Americans Violated Neutrality Act," was a more moderate tone in the L.A. Times.

"Arms Dealers Found in Violation of Arms Embargo", was the headline in the New York Times. "They Sent Military Equipment to Israel in 1948."

This was the ultimate political trial, a hot potato that the judges were reluctant to deal with. The case was tossed from judge to judge until it finally landed in the lap of Peirson Hall, a judge with less seniority than the others. He seemed like a good choice for us, because he was a former Los Angeles council member who ran for a federal senate seat. He also happened to be an aviation buff.

In 1947, the State Department and FBI had carted out and retroactively reinstated the Neutrality Act of 1935, which had been lying dormant for over a decade. Many individuals had over the years found ways to circumvent this Act, and nobody noticed or took action. Suddenly, it had become the biggest crime ever. For the first time, the law was being used in court for the heinous crime of supplying arms and ammunition for the protection of the Jewish state of Israel.

On November 29, 1947, the United Nations voted by a resounding majority to grant independence to a Jewish state in the area known as Palestine. The United States was the first country to cast the ballot in favor. Yet nowhere was there guarantee of protection or support when it became obvious that the Arab states objected and war was inevitable. The United States president, Harry Truman, enforced an embargo on supplying military equipment of any kind to the region. The law bound no other country. The Arabs were getting all they needed from the rest of the world. So, in effect, the embargo on all military equipment to the Middle East at this crucial time prevented only the Jews from getting any help in self-defense. That's what this case was about.

Israel became independent on May 15, 1948. We were indicted on September 30, 1948.

The trial was postponed several times. During this period we were allowed to leave the country for two months for our own purposes.

I was accused of organizing and participating in the smuggling network that defied the Neutrality Act and export control laws. I was charged with allegedly transporting weapons and airplanes and parts stolen from United States ordinance dumps.

HANK GREENSPUN was accused of smuggling military equipment from a base in Honolulu and shipping it to Israel despite the embargo.

ABE LEVINE was accused of selling us B-17 parts and concealing the weapons in his own facilities.

LEO GARDNER was accused of flying an impounded B-17, a heavy 4-engine bomber, out of the country despite the Neutrality Act.

STEVE SCHWARTZ was accused of flying planes loaded with illegal military equipment out of the States to Palestine.

SAM LEWIS, Captain in TWA (Trans World Airways), was charged with flying heavy military equipment to the Middle East through Czechoslovakia despite the embargo by the American government.

WILLY SASNOW was accused of smuggling heavy equipment from the yards in Honolulu to Palestine, in spite of the embargo.

RAY SALK was accused of concealing the stolen equipment and loading the shipment aboard a ship destined for Palestine via Mexico.

ELYNORE RODNICK was accused of training pilots, knowing of their purpose to smuggle military equipment despite the embargo by the United States government.

That's what the public knew: they were all Americans, they were all young, they had all participated in the war against the Nazis as combat fighters, navigators, radio operators, and mechanics. They were all officers in the military, veterans of World War II. And they admitted to defying the American embargo issued by the President of the United States. That meant that, unlawfully and knowingly, we conspired and agreed together to obtain and cause a large number of aircraft and component parts and accessories to be flown from the United States to the Republic of Panama, Czechoslovakia, Italy, and other foreign places to Israel.

I was living in Israel in 1948 when I was served the summons to appear in court in California to face trial for the conspiracy to violate the Neutrality Act and export control law. Case number 20636 of the district court central division of California, U.S. Code Title 18 section 88 for the crime of disregarding the embargo imposed by the United States on military equipment to the newly recognized state of Israel.

Israel did not have an extradition treaty with the U.S., and I could have stayed away, in hiding. I couldn't see myself as a fugitive from my country, my homeland, and decided to return to the U.S. to face the trial. No matter what the outcome would be, that was the only right thing to do.

I had a long-standing relationship with David Ben-Gurion, who had been the leader of the Jewish people, and after the declaration of Israel's independence, he was elected as the first Prime Minister. I told David Ben Gurion of my decision, and he made no effort to talk me out of it. He understood my loyalty and love for my country. Ben Gurion promised me the best lawyers that money could buy in appreciation for all I had done for Israel. In return, I promised him that if I would be sent to jail, I would spend the time learning Hebrew. That was our standing joke. He kept his side of the bargain. I didn't. Ben Gurion was concerned that the American government would be determined to make an example of me, and would sentence me to the maximum term according to the law. He got me the best legal counsel, Bill Strong, Isaac Pacht, and Irwin Margolis. They even anticipated that since I was the main felon, the government would want to make a deal and "trade me in" as the sole "criminal" in exchange for suspended sentences for Charlie Winters and the others.

I flew into Mexico. Near the American border I was met by former judge Isaac Pacht, two U.S. Marshals, two FBI agents, policemen, and my lawyers, Bill Strong and Irwin Margolis. They drove me to LA, unshackled.

2
THE TRIAL

Until the trial began, we were free to carry on with our lives, within limits. I visited my family in Bridgeport. We could not leave the country. With a trial hanging over our heads, we were unemployable. Our accountant, Nahum Bernstein, claimed, "The American system will not convict you if they see the justice in what you were doing." No matter what indictments the government would issue, the jury would see our actions as a matter of compassion, necessity, and justice. I certainly hoped so. We did nothing to endanger American security. All we did was protect a friendly nation from hostile surrounding armies.

We were given rooms at the famous Hollywood Hotel but were too troubled to be able to enjoy the amenities, the pools, the drinks at the bar, and the luxurious conditions. We spent hours with Isaac Pacht and Bill Strong, who were not at all optimistic.

This state of limbo, with a permanent lump coiled in the pit of my stomach, waiting to see what would happen, flashed me back to a harrowing experience I had as a flight engineer on one of the Atlantic crossings during World War II, flying over enemy territory. I looked out the cockpit window, and there, alongside me, was an enemy plane, a Junker 88, the most feared fighter in the Nazi fleet. I could see the pilot's face turned towards me. With a hostile look, he flew closer to our C-54 and shadowed us for a while. Our eyes met. A huge lump of tension and fear filled the pit of my stomach. I was expecting a barrage of shots. Was he about to blow me up into smithereens? I didn't know now what the outcome of the trial would be. But he simply took off. He was as keen to stay alive as I was.

When the trial was about to begin, two FBI agents, several federal marshals, and an entourage of lawyers escorted me into the courthouse in LA. The trial began at 10 a.m. on October 25, 1949, about 15 months after Israel's declaration of independence. In the courthouse I met up with my friends, my "fellow conspirators", who had participated with me in the crimes we were accused of. We were all led to the fifth floor. We pled not guilty. We did not deny the fact that we smuggled planes and military equipment, as charged. We each posted bail of $10,000, which the State of Israel paid. And for weeks we consulted with our lawyers in preparation for the trial.

Every seat in the courtroom was filled.

The top man of the justice department in Los Angeles, Prosecutor James Carter, came only for show, and the next day was sworn in as judge. This just showed how important this trial was to the government. He then relinquished that position to Judge Peirson Hall.

The prosecutor was Robert Kelleher. During jury selection, he made sure that none of the potential jurors would be affiliated with Judaism in any way. All those with Jewish sounding names were eliminated. All efforts were made to find unbiased jurors and to weed out bigots. They wanted a fair-minded jury. The prosecutor wanted to select a jury that would not be prejudiced for or against Jews, or so he said. I tried to read the faces of the jurors. Hank surreptitiously pointed out one juror, and whispered to me, "This one is going to hang us."

We were all tried separately. I was charged with orchestrating and participating in smuggling airplanes and other military equipment to Israel, violating the embargo, the "biggest military smuggling operation in the history of the U.S.," my home country.

Our lawyers contested the moral legitimacy of the laws. There was no criminal intent. We did not endanger American security. We had acted to defend our allies, people under merciless attack by invading armies.

Press releases used such words as "miscarriage of justice" and "aid given to the victims of aggression."

When I took the stand, I said that I took full responsibility for all that we had done. I recruited the rest of the defendants to participate in the acts we were convicted of. I had many aliases.

The attorneys addressed us by our military ranks: Major Greenspun, Lieutenant Schwimmmer, perhaps to acknowledge that we were all loyal Americans who had risked our lives to serve our country during World War II.

As all the witnesses were interrogated, and testified for and against us, a clear picture of the operation evolved. Not only what we had done, but why. Throughout the trial, there were blatant anti-Semitic undertones. The prosecutor kept calling us "these people" in a very derogatory way.

8,000 pages of documents were presented as evidence by the prosecution: bills of purchase that had been stolen from my office, payroll records, transcripts of bugged telephone conversations, intercepted telegrams, hotel registrations, photographs, checks made out to me. The accusations that Greenspun was getting 10 percent commission for all the equipment were unfounded and not substantiated.

A parade of 50 witnesses testified, substantiating their stories with bills of lading and invoices for purchases of airplanes and airplane parts.

The prosecutor tried to convince the jury that we were somehow connected with the Soviet Union. This was the worst accusation possible. After being allies fighting the Nazis during World War II, the Soviet Union was now a mortal enemy of the United States. At the time, the McCarthy era, any connection with the Soviet Union was considered treason, and anything connected with the Soviet Union was under suspicion and distrusted. We had to repeat over and over again that we had nothing to do with communism or the Soviet Union. We also had to insist that we did not betray our country or side with the enemy.

Several of my mechanics from Burbank and a few of my suppliers had become informants. Some were subpoenaed. Others came forward on their own to settle scores over real or imaginary slights.

We were betrayed by one of our own mechanics, Charles Phillips. He was the first witness for the prosecution on the stand, and he testified that I had hired him to work on the C-46 at Millville and then sent him to Zebra, Czechoslovakia, behind the Iron Curtain, where he was surprised and shocked to see the same C-46s. He claimed that in Czechoslovakia he saw disassembled Messerschmidt planes loaded onto the C-46 in crates marked "glassware." That was a lie. We had never sent him to Czechoslovakia, and that country was not behind the Iron Curtain. Our defense lawyer claimed angrily that there was nothing illegal in shipping anything from Czechoslovakia to any other part of the world, regardless of what they contained. Neither Czechoslovakia nor any other country was bound by the American embargo. Connecting these planes with breaking the American law was meant only for the purpose of inflaming the jury.

Another witness for the prosecution was Bill Zadra, who had worked as a mechanic in Burbank. He admitted stealing the papers from my office. Mercenary pilot James Beane also testified against Charlie Winters and me and the rest. For his hostile testimony, he hoped to get a job — a respectable one that pays — at the time when many pilots were out of work.

Another witness, a broker who had been hired to ship the spare engines from LA to Panama, backfired as a prosecution witness when he described how the men had gone through all the legal channels, checking that the engines were not on the list of prohibited exports, and filing the proper customs declarations.

A report was displayed claiming that the Italian police had stopped the loading of 40 tanks into a Panamanian freighter bound for Israel. Again our lawyers intervened, claiming that the Americans had no say over cargo being shipped from Panama to Italy, or from Italy to Palestine. The jurors who heard this looked at us with suspicion.

We all tried to make the court understand the circumstances in Palestine, how frantic and desperate the Jews were, knowing that they were under threat of destruction, with no military ground or air defense. Our mission was to acquire arms for the Jews in Palestine, who were constantly attacked by the Arabs and threatened to kill them all if they created their own state. We knew that the moment the British pulled out of Palestine, all hell would break loose. We were working against time. We knew that the embargo placed by the American government on military equipment to the Middle East affected only the Jews, since the Arabs were getting all they wanted from everywhere else. So the only way we could help would be by smuggling and arming the Jews.

Our defense lawyer, William Strong, decided to go on the offensive. He reminded the jury that his clients had served in the United States military during World War II. They did not avoid their duty to the United States and voluntarily showed up to face trial. They were all Americans imbued with the national tradition of fair play. The defendants rallied to the defense of people who stood unarmed against five foreign armies bent on destroying them. Those same Americans had lost family members during the unimaginable horrors of the Holocaust.

It seemed that all that the prosecutor wanted was facts. Dry facts. He didn't care why, just what. The defense attorney's objections were frequently dismissed. And the fact was that we had broken the law, and admitted it, and had to face the consequences.

But during cross-examination, as more details and information surfaced, facts even beyond what the prosecution was aware of, sentiments prevailed largely for us, the defendants, who had come of our own accord.

By now, a more aggressive prosecutor named Herschel Champlin had replaced the original prosecutor. He had prepared his case very thoroughly.

The jurors and spectators admired us for our participation in the cause of a small, outnumbered country fighting the surrounding armies for its very existence. At the time, we were all unemployed.

After all the other defendants and witnesses were interrogated, the prosecutor pulled out his trump card. He called upon his chief witness for the prosecution.

Nathan Liff was undeniably the star of the show. The prosecutor showed him a photograph and asked whether he knew the man.

Liff said 'yes, this is Hank Greenspun.'

"Do you see him in the courtroom?"

Liff pointed at Greenspun. The prosecutor continued, 'Did you sell military equipment to Mr. Greenspun?'

'No,' said Liff.

The judge reminded Liff, "You are still under oath."

The prosecutor repeated, "So, Mr. Liff, I'm asking you again, did you sell the parts to Mr. Greenspun?"

"No, no, no," said Nathan in his heavy Yiddish accent. "I didn't sell him no nothing."

"Then what was he doing at your salvage yard in Hawaii?" snapped the prosecutor.

"He came to visit, to look 'round, to see if there was maybe something he could use."

The prosecutor demanded, "How did all these engines end up at Schwimmer Aviation?"

Liff repeated, "No, I didn't sell him nothing. I gave it to him as a present."

A gasp, and then laughter broke out in the courtroom. Liff continued: "I knew what they needed it for, and they had no money. Today it's new, tomorrow it's junk. I'm in the junk business. That's why I'm here where the junk is. I knew everything would be melted down because it was surplus and no longer needed by the American military. I told them to take it away, to take what they needed." Then he added, "And I would do it again."

He told the prosecutor that he knew we were not taking them for personal gain; they were essential for the survival of Israel. In Honolulu in 1946, his company, Universal Airplane Salvage Company, won the lucrative War Access Administration contract to dispose of vast stocks of surplus war material including aircraft spare parts. The company dismantled surplus naval aircraft and melted the aluminum into ingots at a junkyard inside one of the naval air stations. He felt that since they were useless to the American armed forces and doomed to be melted down anyway, they could be turned to better use by us. He said to Greenspun, "Whatever you find here, you are welcome to it."

In a very emotional testimonial, he spoke about the murder of his own family members at the hands of the Nazis in Europe during World War II. He felt he had to do his part in creating a Jewish state so this could never happen again.

After all the evidence had been presented and the jury was done deliberating, one juror, Marshall Chlavin, held out against a guilty verdict. This was the juror who we thought would hang us.

Three times the jurors returned to deliberate, and the same juror stuck to his objection to convict. The judge called him to his chambers and said this could cause a mistrial, costing the government a lot of money and wasted time. The juror explained his view. These were not criminals. There was no treason, no harm done to their country. They were breaking the law, but they were fighting for justice, for the right of a small nation, a persecuted people, to survive and live in peace and security.

The judge asked what it would take to have the juror change his vote, and the juror said, "Let's make a deal." The judge countered, "It's not your place to make a deal with a judge. Now, what is it you want?" "Leniency," pleaded the juror. "No prison term for the defendants fighting for their cause." The deadlock was broken.

He returned to the deliberation room, and changed his vote. The guilty verdict was now unanimous.

Greenspun turned himself in and pled guilty. Judge Peirson M.Hall said, "It is one of the most serious crimes because these things you dealt with were used to kill innocent people in a war." Really? Innocent people. Killed in a war. Had never been known to happen in any previous war, certainly not by Americans.

But knowing the motives that impelled him, the judge couldn't bring himself to send Greenspun to prison. Instead, he fined him $10,000, which the Israeli government paid.

Sam Lewis also pled guilty. He was interviewed in one of the newspapers. He claimed he had never flown to Czechoslovakia behind the Iron Curtain. And he clarified that the Iron Curtain stopped in Poland, so the charges against him were wrong. He even produced a map of Europe to demonstrate the borders of the Soviet Union and the Iron Curtain.

I was found guilty of masterminding the entire scheme and recruiting others to break the American law. I was fined $10,000, which the Israeli government paid, and was stripped of all my civil rights, including the right to vote, the basic right of all citizens in a democratic society, and employment in any government capacity. I lost my war veterans' benefits. I was sure that consequently I would never be able to be hired by any airline.

Leo Gardner and Ray Salk were found guilty, fined $10,000 as well, and also deprived of their civil rights.

Abe Levin was charged with selling spare parts for the B-17s. He was later dropped from the case, along with several other people, whom the feds couldn't pin down.

The jury acquitted Willie Sasnow and Sam Lewis. Sam was abroad at that time.

Charlie Winters, who sold us three B-17, was charged separately in Miami, Florida. The prosecutor asked him why he, a non-Jew, was involved. Was it for money? No, replied Charlie, "I am Irish, and I hate the British. I am aware of where my B-17s were destined for." This "righteous gentile" whose "crime" was not nearly as heinous as ours, was slapped with an 18-month sentence in jail.

I was outraged at the gross injustice of the verdicts for a situation that arose only because of the discriminatory law created by the United States government that imposed the embargo in the first place. Justice and the law aren't always on the same page.

But we were free. We were unemployable.

3

A CHILD'S DREAM

know what I want to do when I grow up. I want to build airplanes." That was the decision I made when I was 11 years old.

Growing up during the Great Depression, there was never enough food on the table or extra money for toys or books. My greatest joy was to ride the bicycle that I had made from scraps of metal to the Avon field in Connecticut and watch the pilots fly their planes.

Sometimes the guards would let me past the gate, and the pilots were very kind to this dowdy little boy who spent hours goggling with fascination at the planes. I would come up close to the planes, and the pilots would talk to me.

Sometimes they would take me up into the air with them. It was the most thrilling thing that I could possibly experience. I wanted to fly, too. Al Schwimmer, the pilot. Sometimes I helped them to repair the planes by handing them the wrenches, and cleaning the parts, or using a grease gun to shoot lubrication into the engines. They gave me a big curved needle, the kind they used to sew the canvas onto the wooden frames of the planes, and I treasured it for the rest of my life.

I helped supplement the family income by delivering papers and magazines every morning before school.

My father, John, was very strict and rigid, a disciplinarian, as could be expected from a man of Austro-Hungarian origin with a stronger Jewish identity than mine. Though he wasn't very religious, he did not hesitate to punch anyone who denigrated the Jews. He came from an illustrious Jewish family that did not fare nearly so well in European high society of the 20th century. His mother died when he was young. John's father wanted nothing to do with him, and he was shuffled around from family to family, until he was finally loaded on to a boat and packed off on a one-way ticket to America in 1901. He was 15 years old. Unskilled laborers were roaming the streets of New York City. He took on odd jobs to survive. He later married another Hungarian immigrant named Fannie. Three daughters and a son completed the family. He supported the family with his horse-drawn pushcart, selling vegetables and sodas, and I would help by shining the horse's hoofs with black shoe polish.

My father and I were not cut from the same cloth. He was a pugilist. He loved boxing. He had hoped that his only son would be just such a macho. But I was a quiet, puny teenager with no interest in physical confrontations. For a while he served as sheriff of Bridgeport, Connecticut during the bootlegging era. My two older sisters, Hanna and Selma, couldn't find a job. My third sister, Roslyn, was much younger. My mother was gentle and true to her beliefs in Jewish religion, values, and traditions. She did not force her views on me. I was the apple of her eye, and she named me Adolph in memory of her younger brother, who was killed fighting for Germany during World War I. My mother sent me to the Heder, the Jewish religious school, to prepare for my bar mitzvah. This was a very important coming-of-age tradition in the Jewish faith, one for which I had to study. I learned the Hebrew letters. I would have learned more if the rabbi hadn't been too much like my father, ranting and swinging at me each time I made a mistake.

I grew up wearing "tsitsiot," the four-cornered traditional garb of religious Jews, and discarded it easily when I began to feel out of place in it, especially when I went to see my friends the pilots at Avon airport.

I got hurt one day playing baseball at school. My leg got so infected that the doctor considered amputation. The doctor considered it. I didn't. No way! Without my leg, I wouldn't be able to fly. We heard that very competent Jewish doctors escaping Germany had come to New York City with advanced medical treatments that were still quite unknown in the United States. A nurse in Bridgeport, the sister of future Israeli Prime Minister Golda Meir, recommended a doctor and raised the money, and my mother took me to him. He saved my leg. The scar along my thigh was where a portion of the infected bone was removed, and the leg then became an inch shorter than the other one. Many years later, I met the doctor by chance, and he remembered me. All throughout my teen years I had to prove to myself and to others that I was strong, despite a damaged leg.

I became a part-time apprentice at the Sikorsky aircraft repair company. I went there every day after school and earned my pittance. In my spare time, I tried to build an airplane under an awning in our backyard out of the scraps of wood and metal that I collected.

When I was 15, I felt that my family needed food more than I needed an education. I dropped out of high school in the 9th grade.

I tried to make some money repairing cars in my parents' makeshift garage but it was not as lucrative as I had hoped. I spent more and more time with my friends at the airport, and understood that there's where my passion lay. After a few odd jobs, and with Sikorsky, where I learned the basics of repairing planes, I left home at the age of 17 for a job in California with Vultee Aircraft Co.

Two of my friends wanted to go with me. Always short on money, we found that the cheapest vehicle to rent was a hearse. We slept in the back, where the corpses usually lie. We took turns driving. At one of the stops for refueling, the attendant opened the door, and out jumped what he thought were three corpses. He turned ghastly white and was so shaken that it took him quite a while to be able to fill the tank for us.

I was passionately dedicated to learning all I could about airplanes. My dream, my ambition, was to one day own my own airplane repair company.

I was one of the few Jewish mechanics at Vultee's. That didn't matter to me. I was an airplane mechanic, and a good one at that. I was always interested in taking things apart and putting them together again. I learned one of the secrets of flying: know your airplane, treat it well, and it will reciprocate; it will be your friend. The money I sent home was sorely needed and greatly appreciated. My father had lost his soft-drink bottling business and took a traveling salesman's job, which barely paid the rent.

In 1938, a year before World War II broke out, the British Air Force submitted a contract to build a large number of B-72 bombers at Vultee's Berryfield factory in Tennessee. I was transferred and became crew chief. Imagine a salary of $50 a week, more than I had ever seen. Shortly after, I was lucky to be back in California with Lockheed Aircraft Company at an even higher salary as a flight inspector on a new fighter that Lockheed was developing for the British — the 322 B, the prototype for the famous B-38. I received my Federal Aviation Administration (FAA) certificate as flight engineer and qualified third pilot and went to work for Trans World Airlines (TWA).

4

WORLD WAR II

When World War II broke out in 1939, I was flight engineer at TWA. I was 22 years old. America was drawn into the war after the Japanese attack on Pearl Harbor in December 1941. TWA was recruited into the Air Transport Command.

I didn't see combat. As a flight engineer, I made more than a hundred crossings over the North Atlantic and South Atlantic oceans. I made more than a hundred takeoffs and landings in London, Marrakech, Tehran, Cairo, Casablanca, and Palestine. The first time we landed in Palestine, all the crew members went to the holy sites in Jerusalem. I stayed behind to bask in the sun on the beach in Tel-Aviv, never dreaming the day would come when I would call this desolate land my home.

I was the "token Jew" in my platoon and overheard a comment once by one of the engineers that, 'actually, it wasn't bad, what Hitler was doing to the Jews.' Someone told him that I was Jewish. He said, 'oh, Al — he's a different kind of Jew.' At the time, I didn't really know what Hitler had done to the Jews, nor that there were "different kinds" of Jews. I didn't know much about anything that was happening beyond my flight missions.

I ferried troops, war supplies, and movie stars on their United Service Organization (USO) tours. I even ferried Marlene Dietrich once, and we invited her into the cockpit.

As a child, I was captivated by the image of Dick Tracy. In the comic books, I followed his feats of bravery and ingenuity. Now I was fascinated by the real stories of valor and resourcefulness of the revolutionary Flying Tigers, a group of skilled young American pilots, adventurers, idealists, and mercenaries, high up in the sky, battling evil. The legendary tales of these pilots were the basis of the John Wayne movies. They gripped my imagination and inspired me.

On a flight carrying Patrick Hurley, former ambassador to China, and transporting President Roosevelt's luggage to the Yalta conference, a violent storm over the Atlantic threatened to bring the plane down. On that flight I managed to extinguish fire on two engines, averting a major catastrophe, and the plane landed safely in Casablanca. When we were back in the United States, I went home and found quite a commotion around my parents' house. Reporters crowded around, interviewing my father. My father, in his ignorance of all things concerning aviation, was expounding on how his son, Al, ferried the president himself, across the turbulent ocean.

"The plane was about to plunge into the water. My courageous son crawled out on the wing of the doomed airplane, extinguished the fire flaming up from the engine, single-handedly." He proudly paraded me through the streets of Bridgeport. Some reporter picked up on this story, somehow believing the ludicrous narrative, and called it The Wing Walker. From then on, my fellow crew members dubbed me "Wing Walker", a nickname that stuck to me for a long time. I was glad to finally return to base. For this courage and ingenuity, I received a medal of honor from the American Air Force.

When Germany surrendered on May 8, 1945 (V-E day, Victory in Europe) and Japan surrendered on September 2, 1945, World War II ended. I returned to civilian life, to TWA. I flew all over the world and picked up experiences along the way. I learned to use chopsticks in China. I played with monkeys in the Amazon jungles. I brought a monkey for my parents in Connecticut; it just couldn't adjust to the cold!

I frequently flew to Europe, and only then did I gradually begin to hear about the atrocities of the Holocaust. Throughout the war, afraid of escalating anti-Semitism, the Jews in America, for the most part, kept a low profile. I was beginning to hear the real stories. I couldn't grasp the magnitude of the crimes that had been committed against my people. My mother's family all lived in Hungary during the war, and she constantly asked me to try and find out what had happened to them. I couldn't at that time. Eventually, during one of my flights to Europe, I visited Birkenau, the notorious death camp adjoining Auschwitz. The Hungarian Jews were the last ones brought to that camp in 1944. I managed to track down a monument listing the names of the victims who had been sent from Hungary to Auschwitz. There I found the names of my mother's parents and siblings. I never told her. I didn't want to break her heart.

5

TURNING POINT IN MY LIFE

On one of my trips home in 1947, I happened to meet a high school classmate from Bridgeport who had become an aviation cadet and flown B-17 missions during the war. I couldn't have imagined that this moment, this chance encounter, would change the course of my life.

Fred Levine told me he had heard through the grapevine of an organization called Haganah, a Jewish defense force named for the Hebrew word for protection or defense. It was illegal in the eyes of the British mandate controlling that part of the Middle East, Palestine. Until then I was completely ignorant of the conflicts in the Middle East. Like I said, politics was not my thing.

I heard for the first time that the British Mandate ruling over Palestine limited the number of Jews they allowed in, and the quota was stringently observed. Anyone caught without the proper entry visa was immediately deported to a camp surrounded by barbed wire, located on the island of Cyprus in the Mediterranean Sea. Haganah was secretly training the Jews to fight Arab attacks against the Jewish settlers. The New York office of the Haganah was trying to get support for their mission to save the destitute survivors of the Holocaust and was looking for ways to smuggle them into Palestine through the British blockade. They were acquiring boats and ships in Italy. Fred himself couldn't help them for health reasons, but maybe I could. He gave me the address of their office. Still devastated by what I had heard about the Holocaust, I knew that there must be something I could do. I thought that I might be the person they were looking for, someone who understood airplanes to help them smuggle the refugees into Palestine by air, more safely and quickly.

The Haganah offices were operating from a room in Hotel Fourteen in New York City. They were desperate for help and money from the Jews in America. This was a well-guarded place.

When I walked in, I had no idea what I was in for. I came in and met Shlomo Rabinowitz, head of operations. He was an ex-major in the British army, decorated for action in Africa and Italy. I introduced myself as Al Schwimmer.

"Al?" said Shlomo. "Short for Albert? Alfred?"

"No," I answered, "Adolph, Al for short."

It sounded so harsh, so German. An awkward name for a Jewish boy after World War II. I was immediately under suspicion. I explained that I was named after my uncle, my mother's brother, who was killed as a German soldier during World War I. Shlomo bombarded me with questions. "What are you doing here? Why did you come? What's in it for you?"

I said I was there because I felt I could help. I was asked to come back. I kept coming back again and again to Hotel Fourteen. I was interviewed over and over again, and people were sent to Bridgeport, to find out who these Schwimmers were.

The Haganah was raising money from Jewish donors and benefactors to help the survivors of the Holocaust reach Palestine and to buy military equipment. They started coming up with anything valuable. The owner of a New Jersey amusement park collected thousands of guns in mint condition; a Hollywood screenwriter loaded up his garage with arms; a distant relative from Bridgeport filled a 40,000 square foot former canning factory in Brooklyn with illegal weapons and packed crates full of cans labeled 'fruit preserves' that actually contained gunpowder. How to transport these past the British blockade was the problem.

What Shlomo really wanted were boats and ships. When I talked to him about airplanes, he didn't believe it could be done.

I began to understand Shlomo's apprehension and concerns. People were donating stuff in droves. Were they trying to feel good about doing something? Or did they actually believe there was value in the rusty pistols from World War I? I tried to explain and convince him that a far more efficient and safe way to bring the immigrants into Palestine was by plane. That's where I came in.

I was finally accepted and trusted. The Haganah gradually began to see me as one of them, beyond suspicion. And I had an American passport, which enabled me to travel around freely.

A short time later, Teddy Kollek, a survivor of the Holocaust, replaced Shlomo. Kollek was a tall, handsome man from Austria, a wartime British intelligence officer, who, years later became the illustrious mayor of Jerusalem and held that position for many terms.

I was sent by Kollek to meet Yehuda Arazi for the first time. At that time, his alias, among many others, was Albert Miller. A charismatic man, energetic and resolute, the previous chief of police in Haifa, took on the challenge of organizing the illegal "immigration" of Jews into Palestine under the nose of the British blockade. I convinced him that airlifting the refugees was safer and faster than sending them by boat.

Now that ways had been set up and organized to smuggle shiploads of refugees from Italy, Arazi turned to another pressing need. It was important to acquire planes, which could then be used to create a future air force. But he also saw the need to send arms and ammunition to the Jewish settlers in Palestine who were constantly attacked by the Arabs. He also knew that I was the man he could count on to do everything possible to acquire the appropriate transport planes.

I told him which planes I considered appropriate. The Constellations, created by Lockheed, were the fastest, biggest transport planes in the world. Yehuda wanted to know how I planned to acquire them. I said I was flexible to any opportunity that would avail itself. I knew that the military were selling their surplus planes and that the Lockheed Constellation that cost the army $250,000 was now being sold by the War Assets Administration for $15,000. The airplane I favored most, the C-46 Curtis Commando, could be purchased for $5,000. I asked Arazi how many planes he wanted to buy. We looked at each other and read each other's mind. He knew nothing about aviation, and I knew nothing about rifles. His main concern was how to pay for all we needed. We would both learn as we went along. Eventually it became apparent that money was not an obstacle to Arazi. He gave me a list of planes he coveted. Arazi introduced me to his accountant friend, Nahum Bernstein. I didn't know then what a big part of our operations he would become.

The entire Jewish population of the world was on high alert in anticipation of the vote on November 29, 1947, on whether the independent State of Israel, a homeland for Jews, would be declared.

On November 29, 1947, the United Nations General Assembly voted by a resounding majority for the creation of the independent Jewish state on the ancient site of Israel, alongside the Arab state. The United States vote was the first one cast, and it was in favor. The date of the end of the British Mandate was set for May 14, 1948. A map was drawn up dividing Palestine into two separate states: an Arab state on the west bank of the Jordan River, to be called Jordan, and the Jewish state on the east side, to be called Israel. The Arab population resented living next to an independent Jewish state and threatened to destroy them the moment the Jewish settlers declared the independence of the State of Israel. War between the Arabs and the Jews was inevitable once the British pulled out of Palestine.

The Haganah was training to fight for and defend the creation of the Jewish state. David Ben-Gurion was busy forming military strength, an air force, and a government.

Fearing that the creation of a Jewish state would antagonize the Arab world, and might even cause the Soviet Union to set foot in the Middle East, and help either the Jewish state or the Arabs, the CIA warned President Truman of potential danger. They advised him to stay out of it and revive the Neutrality Act, which had been dormant for a decade, to forbid sending any kind of military equipment to the Middle East. Reluctant to get drawn into another war, this time fighting against their former ally, the Soviet Union, President Truman solved the situation by slapping an arms embargo on the region. No military equipment of any kind to the Middle East. No one in America must help them under penalty of jail. For a decade the Neutrality Act had been violated and ignored by entire industries — including airplane manufacturers — and nobody noticed. The Flying Tigers circumvented the law by renaming the company. Clyde Pangborn, my childhood hero, broke the American law when he joined the Royal Air Force to help fend off the Nazi onslaught in the Battle of Britain.

Other countries, including Arab states, untethered by these laws, could provide the Arabs with all that they requested. The British were openly on the Arab side. The embargo would in fact affect only the Jewish settlers. The Jews were alone. The population of this new and very weak nation was in danger of being massacred.

6
PREPARING FOR A JEWISH STATE

Arab acts of aggression against the Jewish community increased immediately. To end the British mandate, the troops began preparation for departure.

Ben-Gurion's goal was clear: after the British mandate, the local Arabs would be unable to prevent the inflow of immigrants in large numbers, changing the demographics in the region. The Jewish state would be created. He understood that in the end, guns, not the United Nations, would define the borders of the independent Jewish state. The Jews needed guns, ammunition, and most of all, planes. Air supremacy was paramount to the outcome of the war. It was imperative for Israel to be strong, to have aerial dominance, as well as ground forces. It was essential for the very survival of the Jewish people in face of the inevitable attack by the Arab armies when the State of Israel was declared. 600,000 Jews had to withstand millions of hostile Arabs surrounding them.

As the British left Palestine, they damaged all the planes in their bases, presumably to make sure that they wouldn't fall into Jewish hands. As soon as the bases were vacated, the Haganah youth secretly disassembled damaged planes and brought them to their own camps and put them together. These were the forerunners of the Israeli Air Force, called "air service" at that time. Egyptian planes flown by British pilots regularly bombed Tel-Aviv, until one day, out of nowhere, three Egyptian planes flying over Tel-

Aviv were confronted with two Israeli Spitfires. A dogfight ensued, and two Egyptian planes fell into the sea. The third one limped back to its base in Egypt. That put a stop to the daily strafing. These Spitfires were the first two planes of the future Israeli Air Force, flown by American volunteers, who formed the core of the future Israeli Air Force. One of the pilots who downed the Egyptian planes said later that he'd never flown a plane like that, patched together from bits and pieces, but he was told to fly and fight, and he had to do what he had to do.

Thousands of volunteers from abroad came, bringing their skills and dedication, to fight for the creation of the Jewish homeland. They were predominantly Americans, Jews and non-Jews, and from Canada, Australia, South Africa, and other countries. Pilots, mechanics, engineers, doctors, and nurses were all grouped as MACHAL. The name was translated from Hebrew, Mitnadvei Hutz La'Aret, meaning volunteers from abroad. Though the United Nations had voted by a resounding majority for the creation of the state of Israel, to actually implement the dream of a safe and independent homeland for the Jews, it was entirely up to the tiny Jewish population of 600,000 in Palestine, surround by millions of people in hostile countries bent on destroying it. No country was ready to defend it — only Machal.

The Haganah office was set up in Hotel Fourteen and was frantically recruiting volunteers and trying to acquire military equipment. Teddy Kollek's unofficial office was a drugstore across the street from Copa Cubana Nightclub. Knowing that the office in Hotel Fourteen was under constant surveillance, he always carried a heavy leather satchel with coins and tokens for public phones. There he could make and receive calls without fear of being tapped. Calling all over America, he planned and carried out his clandestine operations.

One day, he needed to deliver a large sum of money at the New York seaport. He spotted a young man, a singer at the Copa Cubana, coming out of the nightclub. He approached him, introduced himself, and asked whether the young man would do him a favor. He explained that the FBI was outside, but that he needed someone to take a grocery bag full of money, to a specific person at the seaport. Teddy couldn't do it himself, knowing that the Feds were watching out for him. He said that he was a Jew, and explained that the money was needed for the creation of a Jewish state. The young singer was Frank Sinatra. He obliged Teddy, and delivered the money. Despite Sinatra's reputed connection with the Italian mafia, not a penny was missing from the bag. Teddy and Sinatra became lifelong friends.

I was swept into this cause. I was committed to help the Jews in Palestine. I began to look for ways to procure surplus airplanes and spare parts that were no longer in use in the American Air Force and to have them transported to the Jews in Palestine. The Haganah was secretly training soldiers. They relied heavily on volunteers from abroad with any military expertise. They were especially desperate for pilots and airplanes to gain air dominance. That's where I belonged.

This was my dilemma. I was an ardent patriot, loyal to my country, America. I recognized and appreciated the benefits and possibilities that enabled me to reach for my dreams. I was proud of my country, of its values, heroism, the fight for freedom and democracy throughout its history. I was grateful for the possibilities it opened to me.

On the other hand, I couldn't ignore what I found out had happened to my fellow Jews less fortunate than I, to my mother's entire family in Europe, during the Holocaust. Anti-semitism was a fact of life in most parts of the world, even after the war. Jews continued to be persecuted. Unless they had a country of their own, there was no place where they could live in safety and security. I was lucky that my parents were allowed to enter the United States after World War I. Otherwise, my fate would have been the same as many of the Jews who had to remain in Europe.

In 1945, America was facing many difficulties. Unemployment was high. The demobilized soldiers, officers, and pilots couldn't find jobs. That's how I managed to recruit friends who had served with me in the military to join me in my mission. I started with the friends who served with me in the air transport command. They brought more friends. Most of them were Jews.

Some considered their Jewishness an insignificant part of their lives. Many were unemployed. They were Americans fighting for a cause that happened to be Jewish. They were helping in the fight to create a Jewish homeland after the horrendous events perpetrated on the Jews by Hitler's regime. They knew they weren't going to get much of a salary. They wanted to be active again, doing something incredibly important. Jews from all walks of life joined in to help.

7

HOW DOES ONE STEAL AN AIRPLANE?

I was told by a man I was introduced to, Charlie Winters, that there was a B-17 Flying Fortress up for sale in Tulsa, Oklahoma. We needed it desperately. We were in California.

Leo Gardener and I decided to go to Tulsa to buy the plane. At that time, I was "Leonard Burns." Leo was in the process of divorce, and his wife kept him under "house arrest." There was a period in my life when I was dating some nurses who were under curfew from 10 p.m. I used to throw them a rope, pad the seat of my convertible, and they would jump out of the window straight into my car. I reverted to this familiar strategy when picking up the housebound Leo.

Leo and I flew to Tulsa. From there he notified his wife that he would be home in a few days. We went to meet with the owner of the plane. I paid the man a fortune for it. He deposited the check and promptly notified the authorities. The Feds contacted the Tulsa airport and hung a large sign on the nose of the plane, saying "Seized by the United States' government". They gave instructions to move the plane to the military side of the airport.

I discovered this when I went with Leo to the airport to inspect our new purchase. The people at the airport looked at us suspiciously and told us to wait a few minutes.

Leo and I left immediately and returned to our motel. Leo got cold feet and wanted to drop the whole deal. My stubborn streak wouldn't let us, especially since we were so double-crossed. And we had paid for it!

With the help of a friend, with whom I had worked in TWA, who was then working at the airport, we found out that the plane had been moved just next to Hangar 3 at the military base.

The next night, in torrential rain, Leo and I, in our spick-and-span Air Force officer uniforms, took a cab and drove to the base. There happened to be a celebration going on at that time. At the gate, rows of elegant cars were spilling out their passengers. Stepping out of their cars, officers in dress uniform and elegant ladies in gowns and high heels, bundled in rain-coats, scuttled under umbrellas towards a festively lit building. The gate was guarded by a single armed soldier. As our cab driver pulled up and rolled down the window, we could hear laughter and dance music. The young guard asked us whether we were going to the party. Yes, of course we were. He said, "There's so much booze and beautiful chicks. Oh, you'll have a great time."

Leo told the young sentry that there was a plane in one of the hangars that he had flown during the war, and for sentimental reasons he would like to see that plane again, just once. He asked whether the guard would allow the cab to go in and take us to the plane, which was in Hangar 3. He agreed. We drove straight to the hangar. The cab driver was delighted with the $20 tip I gave him, and off he went in the pouring rain.

Sheltered under the wing of our plane, we looked at each other, wondering what to do next. Leo had never flown a B-17. I was not a pilot. We climbed into the plane and fiddled around with the instrument panel. It took a while to figure it out, but we managed to take off.

The bewildered air control officer in the tower asked us to identify our-selves. We kept silent. He saw that we were taxiing and warned us that there was another plane trying to land. I urged Leo to keep going. The other plane had to be directed away to another runway.

The FBI got wind that something strange was going on and alerted all the bases. By that time we were gone, on our way to New Jersey, where Teddy Kollek, Bernstein, and a friend of his, pilot Irvin "Swifty" Schindler were waiting at our prearranged rendezvous. The idea was that Schindler, who claimed to be familiar with B-17s, would fly the plane first to Czechoslovakia, and from there to Palestine.

We appreciated every contact we could make in our efforts to help our cause. Teddy Kollek knew someone who knew someone who knew Manuel Fuentes, a Portuguese Marrano Jew whose family had been forced to convert to Christianity, but furtively remained Jewish. Fuentes lived on the Ozores island of Terceira. This influential businessman's enterprises included the operation of Terceira's airport. He allowed us to land there, which was ideal for our refueling stopovers. For obvious reasons, the stipulation was that we would be in and out in no time. That suited us fine. That would be the route for our plane.

Bernstein warned us to be on the watch for FBI agents, who were on the way to the airport. There was already a bulletin on a missing Flying Fortress on the loose. Though Leo, Teddy, and I were nervous, Swifty took his time. Reporters started showing up and asking questions. What we learned later was that Swifty had never flown a B-17 and was trying to figure it out. By the time he took off, there was a reporter in a plane on his tail.

The FBI was attempting to find a missing war surplus bomber, which was apparently on its way to Israel, warned the media. The Americans sent out the word to airports all over the southern Atlantic. Teddy, Leo, and I immediately returned to New York.

The FBI finally found the missing plane at the Terceira airport in the Azores. They failed to notice that a few days prior, three other similar American airplanes left from Terceira airport to an unknown destination. They seized the plane and sent Schindler and his team back to the States, handcuffed.

Swifty Schindler was tried in New York by a Jewish judge who found him guilty. He was fined $2 and sentenced to one-year probation. The FBI agents complained of political machinations, and the Los Angeles Examiner went so far as to question the judge's loyalty to the United States. Antisemitism in action.

8
LOOKING FOR OPPORTUNITIES

We were constantly on the lookout for new opportunities. In England, Willie Sasnow bought three Bristol Beaufighters in mint condition from the RAF surplus stocks. These were formidable combat aircraft. He established a "motion-picture firm" in London, and the planes were filmed in Kent. On the second day of filming, the Beaufighters took off in formation, with Willie on board, and landed in Israel.

He also bought four A-20, but these, regretfully, were seized by United States customs. By what right? Oh, well. We win a few, lose a few.

I heard that Lockheed in Los Angeles was selling Constellations. I contacted Ray Selk, a friend from Connecticut, who had served with me in the air transport command during the war. We both had a dream that one day together we would have a place of our own. Ray got Willy Sasnow into the venture. Willy was a master mechanic and flight engineer who had worked with me in TWA. We flew to Lockheed at the airport in Burbank, where the Constellations were built. I hungered for them. We browsed around and found out that the War Surplus Administration was selling the surplus Connies and Dumbos for a steal: Connies for $15,000 and C-46 Dumbos for $5,000. The government had acquired a few thousand planes that were not needed anymore. Surplus planes were scattered in airport storages, depots, and literally strewn all over the Arizona desert, as far as the eye could see: C-46s, C-47s, and 54s Constellations, just sitting around for years, rusting in the scorching sun in deserted areas. The government was anxious to get rid of them. They were up for grabs, but not to us. In view of the embargo, we could not get a license to fly them out of the United States. We planned to camouflage the fighter planes as passenger planes, as they would be easier to smuggle out. But we didn't have the funds for that. Ray decided to remain in Laos Angeles and Willy and I had to return to New York to meet with our accountant, Bernstein, and tell him of the treasures we had seen in Los Angeles. We regularly commuted between California and New York, and wherever else was necessary.

I had an idea. I would round up some of my buddies, the mechanics, and we could do it for a fraction of the cost. Bernstein gave me the OK and enough money to start the operation. I flew to Washington, and first thing the next morning, went to the War Assets Administration and bought three surplus Constellations, and 10 Dumbos. What a buy! We rented a hangar at the airport in Burbank, called it Schwimmer Aviation, and set up shop. Selk was in charge in Burbank, while I spent most of the time hopping between the two coasts. Schwimmer Aviation hired 30 to 40 mechanics for $1.80 per hour, which was a very good salary at the time. We oiled the fuselages and wings, rubbed the rust with oil by the barrel, repaired leaking fuel tanks, and faulty landing gears. It took months to make these planes airworthy.

CIA agent Bernard Ptacek paid me a visit and flashed his badge at me. He wanted to know what we were doing at Schwimmer Aviation. I said we're building an airline and bringing it up to FCC standards.

Whoever snooped around was given a spur-of-the-moment story about our operation. I myself couldn't keep up with the stories. Reporters who were trying to get a scoop were soon frustrated and left us alone.

Spare parts were a problem, even more difficult than buying planes. It was taking more time than we had anticipated to assemble the planes. I was forced to buy a fourth Constellation, just to salvage the spare parts.

Suddenly, we had a streak of luck beyond all expectation. A man came to Haganah at Hotel Fourteen in New York, and introduced himself as Nathan Liff, the junk dealer from Hawaii, offering exactly the kind of engines and spare parts that I needed. This was the junk dealer who later testified at our trial. He described a field in Hawaii as half a mile long and a quarter mile wide, stocked with 2000 HP Pratt and Whitney R2800 engines for the Dumbos spare parts, and all kinds of weapons, bullets, and rifles that the Haganah desperately needed. He said that because he was so impassioned by the idea of a Jewish state in Palestine, he traveled all the way from Hawaii to New York and begged to help.

Teddy Kollek tried to reach me with a public phone booth outside Hotel Fourteen; he had incredible news. It took him quite a long time to locate me, wherever I happened to be. I was overjoyed at the possibility of getting the engines and other military equipment. But neither my partners nor I knew anything about rifles and other war materials. We needed a trustworthy expert to come with us. Selk immediately thought of his cousin, Hank Greenspun, from Las Vegas, who had been an officer and company commander in Patton's Third Army throughout the war and was now publisher of a free press newspaper, The Sun, in Las Vegas. Sasnow and I made a quick stop in Las Vegas on our way back to California. We met Hank, and I came straight to the point. We needed his expertise. He was immediately ready to go to Hawaii to check the guns. He was a man of his word.

Hank went with Sasnow to Hawaii to Liff's junk yard piled high with aircraft engines and spare parts, no longer needed by the armed forces, that was to be melted down into nuggets.

"Take anything you need. You are welcome to it. Free of charge," Liff told them.

Greenspun noticed a heavily-guarded Navy arms depot with every imaginable kind of military equipment, hundreds and hundreds of guns, brand-new 50- and 30-calibre machine guns, and ammunition also waiting to be scrapped and melted down into nuggets, all behind Liff's junkyard. What a waste! There were mountains of equipment that were so desperately needed

to save the Jewish state. The Navy depot was separated from Liff's scrap-
yard by a "no-man" strip of ground and heavy amounts of barbed wire. So
as not to implicate Liff in any way, Greenspun bribed his workers to pilfer
the Navy depot at night, when the guards weren't looking and Liff was at
home. They loaded machine guns into crates marked "Engine Parts." Into
T9 crates, each containing 50 guns, he added the shipment of engines and
other airplane parts, to be delivered to me. Liff told the foreman these were
engine parts, and the foreman made the necessary property pass for the
crates to leave the field. For six weeks, Filipino workmen helped to crate the
surplus guns and ammunition and move them to the other side of the fence.

All the crates, with proper invoices, arrived at Schwimmer Aviation. This
proved to be a mistake. It drew attention to the huge shipment. The company came under strict surveillance because one of the mechanics leaked
the story to the FBI. Hank was back in Las Vegas when he got word that
the Feds were suspicious that military equipment was being stolen. Hank
himself came back to California to spirit all these treasures out of our facility. He put out the word for help.

Groups of volunteers, assembled by Bernie Fineman, came to help. Den-
tists, lawyers, a film producer, studio workers, businessmen, people from the
movie industry, and more were asked to do work they were unfamiliar with.
They worked vigorously in shifts for a week, oiling and wrapping the guns,
and stacking them in crates. They lugged the heavy equipment, under cover
of night, and stored them among our friends, in garages, storefronts, base-
ments, and homes, until such time as we would find a way to transport them
to the Haganah in Palestine. Abe Levin was very helpful by storing crates in
his storage facility. That was the charge against him. By the time the Feds arrived, 42 crates were out of my facility and on their way to their destination.

Only during the trial, we found out why the Feds came: Charles Philips,
the mechanic whom I had sent to Millville to work on the C-46's, informed on us. So many crates appearing there aroused his suspicion. He
blithely testified that he had been sent behind the Iron Curtain, where he
was shocked and surprised to see the same C-46's. This was a blatant lie.
He had never been sent behind the Iron Curtain. Hank was not aware of it.

9
NEXT PROBLEM

Our next challenge that needed a solution was transporting the crates unobtrusively. How does one ship all these treasures?

Crises packed upon each other. The Feds were after us; so was the CIA, headed by a man by the name of George Bush. The CIA came up with ordinances to upgrade fuel-injection systems in order to fly passengers, at a cost of $20,000 per engine. I protested. And I stalled. I now had reason to move the entire operation to Central America, out of the jurisdiction of American policy. In Last Vegas, meanwhile, the Feds were trying to track the guns stolen from Hawaii. Two FBI agents paid me a visit. They wanted to inspect the "junk" that we had received from Hawaii. I gave them full access into my facility. Aside from the aircraft engines and spare parts that were out for the taking, they didn't find anything. They checked all the contents of the cargo, grilled me with questions, and left. They frequently sat in their cars on both sides of the field, watching, to make sure we weren't loading contraband material, what they chose to call contraband, on our planes. Their day shifts replaced their night shifts. They couldn't prove that we had taken guns and ammunition. We often waved to them, but they never responded.

All that made us uncomfortable. We had to get everything out of Schwimmer Aviation as urgently as possible, as legally as possible. I desperately needed to somehow get our crates out of America, and then all the way to Palestine.

We were constantly looking for people to join our cause, to help in many different ways. Most of all, we needed pilots. They had to be experienced, adventurous, reliable, and discreet, and sensitive to the horrors of the gas chambers and concentration camps and all that Hitler's regime had done to the Jews in Europe. I began to recruit them. I appealed to their American principle of standing up for the underdog, which in this case was the Jews in Palestine, surrounded by enemies. I needed them immediately. That's when I approached Steve Shwartz, a pilot whom I knew from the war years. He couldn't get work and had almost given up the idea of flying. He was glad to join me in the mission. In our Schwimmer Aviation office in New York, he looked up pilots, aircrew members, and mechanics with Jewish-sounding names and came up with a long list of volunteers.

Ben Gurion's voice was a constant echo in my mind: "We are desperate. We need heavy arms. We don't have any bullets left. We need airplanes."

Now that most of the planes in Burbank were assembled to look like passenger planes, they were ready to go.

Several possibilities were beginning to open up to us. The logistics were complex, and time was of the essence. The Feds were trying to prevent what we were trying to accomplish. The first thing we had to do was get everything out of Schwimmer Aviation in Burbank.

We needed the cooperation of foreign countries and were beginning to find ways of dealing with them.

Arrangements were made to fly our planes to a defunct army air force base with a 5,000-foot long runway in Millville, New Jersey, left over from its days as a United States Air Force base. Four crewmen planning to fly the planes, stopped off in Burbank. I thought Bill Gerson was the best pilot for this mission.

I met the pilots and rushed them to load the airplanes as quickly as possible. They crammed the planes from floor to ceiling with Pratt and Whitney engines, spare parts, and the other treasures that Hank had gotten from the Hawaiian junkyard. I made it as clear as I could that every bolt, every bullet, every spare part was precious; nothing was to be left behind. The pilots flew from Burbank to the airport in Millville, New Jersey. From there, the crates had to be brought to Acapulco, Mexico.

Sam Lewis and crew flew the first plane. He had to clear customs for the trip to Mexico. This was a big test. The customs agent went through the Connie and out again, without seeing anything suspicious. He cleared the plane for takeoff.

The flight plans were complex: stopover in Jamaica to refuel, then Tocumen, and on to Rome — where Arazi had stockpiled supplies from all over Europe, meant to reach the Jews in Palestine as soon as the British pulled. From Rome they went to a remote airfield at Castiglione de Lago. The best-laid plans are not always smooth, and we had to deal with crises and unexpected problems as they arose. Each plane that arrived, each cargo delivered, was a triumph.

Two concurrent plans were being hatched. One route would be through Mexico. The crates with the machine guns, several dozen French 75 mm cannons, thousands of shells and aerial bombs, and several million rounds of ammunition were to be sent from Acapulco by rail to Tampeko on the east coast of Mexico. There they were to be loaded onto a freighter named *Kefalos* that Teddy Kollek had purchased. Greenspun was in Mexico City, negotiating with the authorities to transfer the crates.

I needed a small boat to take the cargo to Acapulco. My friend Natasha introduced me to an actor by the name of Leon Jacobs, better known as actor Lee J. Cobbs. I knew he was Jewish, and I explained what I needed his boat for. He admitted that his boat was too small for our purpose and connected me to his friend, a Jewish yachtsman, Lee Lewis, with a suitable boat, *The Idalia*, that same day. We paid him the $25,000 he asked for, trucked our crates to a nearby marina, and loaded them on *The Idalia*.

Nothing went smoothly. Unexpected crises arose and were dealt with. The batteries on the boat were low. Keys couldn't be found. A night watchman's attention had to be diverted. A group of amateur stevedores dragged the heavy crates from the truck, to the pier, to the boat. The crew worked frantically all night, and at crack of dawn, *The Idalia* sailed off towards Acapulco with Hank aboard. The owner threatened to cancel the deal because of the weight of the cargo exceeded the initial agreement. Hank put a gun to his head and forced him to continue to Acapulco as agreed.

10

MEXICO CITY

We were negotiating with the Mexicans for the purchase of P-47s and had finalized the deal with the Mexican government about transporting our crates to the ship we had acquired. But suddenly, the authorities in Mexico City changed their minds about our "arrangements" and demanded $250,000 more, justifying it by claiming that our cargo needed to be transported under military guard and loaded on to the *Kefalos*. Our man in Mexico, Elias Surasky, immediately notified Teddy in New York.

Teddy assigned me to handle the arrangements with the Mexican authorities in Mexico City. With a briefcase containing $250,000 and a pistol tucked into my belt under my jacket, I went off to Mexico City.

Elias Surasky's Mexican employee met me. On the way to his parked car, I stopped at a window of a gun store. It was very hot. I took out my handkerchief to wipe the sweat off my forehead. Just as I was about to get into the car, I felt a hand on my shoulder. I turned around and faced a Mexican, who spoke to me very rapidly and aggressively in Spanish, which I didn't understand at all. My escort turned white, saying that this man, who was a detective, claimed that he saw through the store window that I had a gun under my jacket. He said a gringo is not supposed to carry a gun in Mexico! I couldn't deny it. He wanted the gun, and I gave it to him. I was afraid that he would want the briefcase as well. My escort calmed me and said if he had wanted it, he would have demanded it by now. The detective hailed a taxi and we all three crowded into the back seat. I was in the middle. I asked where we were going. To the police station, I was told. My escort was very agitated by then. They spoke in rapid Spanish. I knew that if I ever entered the police station, I would never walk out of it alive. I wondered how they would dispose of my body. After a lengthy discussion between the employee and the detective, the taxi driver was told to pull up at the curb, and the employee asked if I had $20 with me. The detective slipped the bill into his pocket, got out of the cab, told us to get out too, and waved the cab driver on his way. The detective went his way, and I went to deliver the contents of the briefcase to the Minister of Defense, who kept his side of the bargain. That was what my life was worth in Mexico: $20! Mission accomplished, I returned to Burbank.

Our crates were on their way to Acapulco aboard *The Idalia*. Shortly after they arrived, the owner of the boat ran to the American consulate with his story, but by then the crates were already on their way elsewhere.

Hank left Acapulco by rail with his cargo of arms and arrived safely in Tampeko. Under Mexican naval supervision, the crates were laden onto the freighter, Kefalos. It sailed off without Hank with several Haganah men aboard. A few months later, it arrived in Haifa, after the state of Israel was created, still desperately needed, at the height of the war for independence. This operation was one of the main charges against Hank Greenspun at the trial. He was also accused of getting 10 percent of the value of the sales, which was a total fabrication.

11
DISASTER IN MEXICO CITY

In Acapulco, four planes were ready for takeoff. Our pilots were already waiting for further instructions when *The Idalia* arrived. The cargo was loaded on the planes to more than full capacity. That was a gamble they took, working against time. They were on their way to Panama City and had to stop in Mexico City for refueling. They arrived at the airport as per plan. I hoped that there would be no more obstacles in our way, but unfortunately, the worst was yet to come, and I wasn't there. After refueling, the planes were ready to go to Panama City. One of planes lifted off, then bumped down on the tarmac, and then managed to take off again. The second plane was not as lucky. Mexico City is at a very high altitude in the mountains. At 17,000 feet above sea level, the thin air atop the mountain range was unable to handle the overloaded plane. It crashed, killing the mechanic, Glenn King, on the spot. The pilot, Bill Gerson, was still conscious when the ambulance came for him, but died on the way to the American hospital. The contents of the plane, and the radio communication equipment, were sprayed all over the runway and had to be collected immediately. The mourning period had to be postponed.

The electronics of the wrecked plane were salvaged and somehow crammed into the other already overstuffed planes.

The men, who had all been given $500 in case of accident, collectively put their money into Gerson's pocket. Norman Moonitz flew to Mexico City in bad weather, flying our C-46 with no oxygen system. Because of this, Moonits was slightly disoriented and made a mistake. The plane slammed onto the runway and destroyed the landing gear. It took two days for the replacement part to arrive and to repair the damage, but Moonitz and this crew were not hurt.

Gerson and King were our first two casualties in the battle for Israel's independence. Could anything have gone differently had I been there?

The remaining planes took off safely for Panama City, as per the plan. From Mexico, planes could legally fly in and out of Panama.

I was in California when I got the devastating news. I went to convey the disastrous message and my condolences to the wives. Gerson's wife, Lillian, blamed me personally; she slapped my face and called me a murderer. She tore up the $10,000 check from her husband's insurance policy and threw it on the ground. I never forgave myself for overloading the planes. The need for arms and the pressure from the Haganah were so great that a fatal accident was bound to happen.

The mechanics in Burbank continued installing auxiliary fuel tanks in the C-46's for the long flight across the ocean. On the manifestos for the Panamanians, they wrote that they were carrying milk and beef.

Swifty Schindler cabled me in the USA and warned me of open insurrection by the remaining crew who were now in Panama City. I flew straight to Panama City accompanied by Hank, Shwartz, and a Haganah man from Chicago by the name of Hyman Schectman to face the rebellious crowd. There were grumbles of discontent: What are we doing this for, the $25 a week or for the glory of Al Schwimmer so the Haganah will say what a terrific guy he is? We volunteer and risk our lives for this?

What a list of grievances I was facing! I was shocked to find out that Swifty Schindler himself was the instigator of the revolt that I was trying to restrain. The pilots didn't know the entire story behind the planes. He should have known better. He should have made them understand. Instead, I was accused of knowingly overloading the planes. I was in no mood to hear this from Schindler, who was very much aware of what was at stake.

"You guys spread the accusation that I'm to be blamed for Gerson's and King's death," I said. A deathly silence followed.

"If you think that the overweight caused the death, I am indeed to blame. Remember, we have had to work around the clock, under extreme difficulty. We did all we could; we did our best. Our 'customers' can't wait much longer. I offer anyone who wants to quit a ticket back to the United States," I continued.

Hyman Schechter spoke next. Everybody wanted to hear what the stranger had to say.

"Call me a friend. Now I want to tell you about our customers. I am one of them. I want to see the cargo you carry to Rome to arrive in my homeland."

He gave a moving account of what was actually happening in Palestine to the attacked Jewish defenders. "The Jews in Palestine are waiting desperately for the planes and equipment. All we have are tiny 40 hp cubs and Austers, Tiger Moths. They aren't even worthy to be called airplanes. You want to know who flies them? Boys from aero clubs, students, and office clerks. But we do have an Air Force, a real Air Force, and you people in this room are it. You American Jews are our air force. Every screwdriver, every cartridge, every gun, that is flown in from the United States, you are the guys who fly them. The Israelis have only antique rifles to defend themselves with, and empty coke bottles that create such a whistling sound when thrown out of a plane that it frightens the Arabs away. You are not flying refugees, or Panamanian passengers, or cattle. That's the story for the Panamanians. You are the beginning of our future air force."

He described in sordid detail the hatred of the Arabs, the cruelty and sadism awaiting the Jews if they lost their fight for an independent country. "I don't intend that my old rabbi friend, who speaks 11 languages and has a number that the Nazis tattooed on his arm in Auschwitz, should die with his head caved in by an Arab rifle butt after his balls have been cut off and stuffed in his mouth."

They needed real planes, flown by experienced fighter pilots.

By the time he was done, the pilots had a new enemy, not me, but the Arabs. One of the mechanics said what was on all their minds, that they had suspected that the cargo was connected with Israel, but nobody said anything, and nobody really cared. I told Schindler that, as of now, he would no longer be in charge, and would be replaced by Auerbach. He had the choice to either stay on as a pilot or go back to the United States. He stayed on as captain and regained my respect. One guy quit. Another was fired by Swifty. The rest all stayed on, convinced that "Al can do the impossible."

We still continued our negotiations with the Mexican deal for the P-47's.

12
THE PANAMA PLAN

Before all this happened, something much more complicated had been set in motion. Bernstein had a sudden spark of inspiration. He was having discussions with his friends in Panama City. These plans were much more intricate. It was necessary to get the crates unobtrusively out of the U.S. planes laden with arms and engine parts that would fly from Burbank to Panama City, and from there to Palestine.

An elaborate plan began to form. Bernstein remembered that his friend in New Jersey, Swifty Schindler, had not long ago opened a charter company named Service Airways. Business was very slow. Swifty had to sell his only plane to cover his debts. All he had left was the name of the company and the certificate of its authenticity. That was exactly what Bernstein needed to pursue his plans. Bernstein shared his idea with Swifty and immediately prepared a contract to use Service Airways as a cover for moving my crates out of the US. Within a day the company was incorporated. Schindler was named president, alias Mr. Schanker. Ray Selk was vice president. Bernstein immediately deposited $50,000 into the newly formed company. Next they approached Schindler's friend, Martin Bellefond, who was an ex-Army Air Force major. He was also Jewish. Bellefond's dream was to have his own airline. He had set up his office in a tent with a pay phone at an airport in New Jersey, from which he offered chartered services to Puerto Rico on a converted C-47 Dakota. He was successful for a while until his lapse in filling the necessary paperwork came to the attention of the CIA.

Bellefond suddenly had a brainwave. If boats could be registered offshore to avoid American red tape, why not airplanes? That concept worked perfectly for us. If our planes could legally reach Panama, they would not be subject to the U.S. arms embargo. With Panamanian registration numbers on their wings, the planes could then fly anywhere. Why not to Palestine?

Bellefond approached an influential Panamanian. The timing was perfect. The Panama government had decided to build an airport in Tocumen, which would cost a fortune. There was a lot of opposition to this project, because there were practically no flights in and out of Tocumen. Bellefond was hoping to get valid registration for his plane and to get a franchise for the national airline of Panama, to be named Lineas Aereas Panameñas Sociedad Anonima (LAPSA), based in Tocumen. It would enable him to cut out the paperwork in America and create the Panama airline, a status symbol, at the same time. Service Airways would lease airplanes of any nature and description to LAPSA. The Panamanians were told there would be regular scheduled passenger and cargo service, but the bureaucratic red tape took so long that Bellefond lost his company and his one plane in the United States. Yet he managed to hang on to the Panama deal. Bellefond and Bernstein had to readjust their plans so that planes flying to Panama would not be subjected to scrutiny. The American authorities would have no problem allowing planes to fly to Panama. Some of the planes that had been legally acquired would fly directly from Schwimmer Aviation in Burbank to Panama. And planes legally registered in Panama would be able to fly to anywhere in the world. A Haganah agent met with me in New York, bringing a roll of microfilm concealed in his underwear, maps of hidden airfields in orange groves outside of Tel-Aviv, a list of secret codes, and a plan of action. Selk and his men in Burbank had to finish preparing the planes and fly them to the small airport in Millville, New Jersey. All we needed were qualified, reliable, and discreet pilots. A tall order, but we found them.

We would then have to transfer the crates in our planes from Burbank, Schwimmer Aviation legally out of the United States. The crates were marked "engine spare parts", "sugar", and "oranges".

Just as things seemed to be running smoothly, we were faced with another predicament. In mid-March, in the wake of the communist coup in Czechoslovakia, President Truman plugged the flow of any American military equipment to troubled areas, including aircraft weighing over 35,000 pounds — effective April 15.

We were racing against time, with crisis after crisis added on.

In Millville, Leo Gardner was preparing the pilots for their mission. It would be a night flight, no formation, no lights, and no radio contact. They would follow the lights of the Philadelphia, Baltimore, Washington, D.C., and Richmond airports, and then hug the coastline all the way to Central America.

Using Schwimmer Aviation planes to fly to Panama was not against American law. The Schwimmer Aviation sign on the office door in New York was replaced with Service Airways (Swifty's licensed aircraft company), and the Panamanian airline named LAPSA would finally be created. With elections just months away, the presence of the airline could tip the scale for the president's reelection. Voters would see that the airline could be profitable and Tocumen would benefit. Regular scheduled passenger and cargo service were promised. LAPSA airline would be a status symbol. On February 15, the deal was clenched. Bellefond rented space for a ticket office and accommodations for the crew. He created a logo for LAPSA for publicity. Both Bernstein and Bellefond knew that the destination of our planes was Palestine, for the Haganah. But the Panama authorities did not. After months of preparation, everything was ready.

Our company was under constant surveillance by U.S. treasury agents, who were suspicious of our motives. Our pilots would wave to them, sitting in their cars in their overcoats and hats, the typical undercover snoopers.

Schindler was in Millville, and I was in the Service Airways office in New York when the phone rang at 3 a.m. An official supposedly from the Treasury Department wanted to talk to me. They didn't believe the LAPSA story and forbade us to fly. I ignored the order. We had come too far to stop an hour before our scheduled takeoff.

Meanwhile, in Millville, customs agents, federal marshals, and treasury agents blocked the runways with their cars, preventing our planes from leaving.

Swifty went to talk to the head man, Ralph Fisher, who told him that we were under suspicion of carrying contraband, and our planes were forbidden to fly. Fisher said that the numbers on the planes identified them as American and needed government clearance to leave the United States. It's true; our crew had forgotten to paint over the American registration numbers with Panamanian numbers. Shoving a pack of documents at Fisher, mostly in Spanish, Swifty was out to prove that these planes actually belonged to a Panamanian company. Swifty pleaded, "We didn't have a chance to change the registration numbers." A simple layer of paint will resolve the issue, but Fisher wouldn't allow our men to drive their cars off the tarmac.

Swifty sent a mechanic to a nearby hardware store for paint, and with the help of ladders from the hangar, the Panamanian registration numbers were put on the planes. The sloppy job, with wet paint dripping down, letters bleeding into numbers, was enough to allow the planes to take off. Swifty showed the Treasury agents that now the planes were Panamanian. The agents smirked and drove away.

At some point, U.S. Customs impounded the two Constellations that were still being worked on in Burbank, but somehow overlooked the rest of the planes, and they all managed to fly out.

Meanwhile back in New York, I called Bernstein who in turn called the State Department in Washington, threatening that they had no legal grounds for stopping the planes, and they would have to use force. That would lead to a congressional investigation, and cause a scandal. He then called me back and said the planes were safe for takeoff. I called Gardner in Millville, and he in turn told Swifty, who gave the order to the Dumbo pilots to fly. Fisher hysterically yelled at them to stop, by order of the government, prohibiting them from leaving, but who listened? Auerbach, Moonitz, Schindler and Raab took off towards Panama.

All throughout this operation, I was afraid that at any given moment the Panamanian government would catch on, and we'd all find ourselves in a jail cell. Teddy Kollek said he hoped the Panamanians could take a joke; I doubted it. And forgiveness? Forget about it!

Five days later, on April 13, just before Truman's embargo took effect, the rest of the planes in Burbank took off for Panama.

In Panama, the aircrew prepared and trained for the next leg of the flight: Panama to Italy, where other Haganah personnel were ready to prepare the planes for their final destination. There was camaraderie and unity among the men, and they enjoyed all the entertainment the city offered in the evenings.

The Panamanians were preparing for the inaugural flight of the newly formed LAPSA airline. They were totally ignorant of the real deal behind the deal. Even Bellefond was not in on the entire clandestine plan. He hoped that LAPSA would really be a legitimate airline, flying all over the world, so an occasional detour to Palestine could be overlooked. Pepsi-Cola Company saw this as an opportunity to get a foothold in Panama, and hired LAPSA for an inland flight.

A few days later, eight Dumbos with three people per plane arrived in Panama. There was a lot of preparation before the flight to Palestine could take place. Mechanics checked the engines, crews had to make sure that the loads were balanced in the holds, and several refueling stops planned in detail. It was imperative to make sure that everything was in order before departure. The first leg of our secret destination was Brazil. From there, across the Atlantic, on to Casablanca, Rome, and Palestine. Very stringent and careful preparations had to be made without attracting any attention. One empty Connie was a dismantled training airplane, with the idea of fitting it with bombing racks and turning it into a dive-bomber. The crew members had to hone their skills and acquire new ones as needed.

To distract the Panamanians, we loaded a few planes with oranges and flew them around Panama, just for show. I told Bellefond to spread the message that the entire fleet would be flying out to explore different international flight routes.

One week after the disaster in Mexico City, five LAPSA planes with Panamanian flags were scheduled to take off on "route survey flight," as Bellefond explained it to his Panamanian associates, to evaluate the most practical routes to Europe for LAPSA passenger and cargo service. In truth, the planes were meant to take off from Tocumen to Brazil to Palestine.

On May 8, 1948, one week before the Declaration of the Independence of Israel, a great celebration took place, complete with many important guests, speeches, and a ribbon-cutting ceremony. Dignitaries showed up at the airport to wish the pilots good luck. A brass band started off with the Panamanian national anthem, and photographers took pictures for the local newspapers. Elegant ladies in their large hats and exquisite attire sat in anticipation on the VIP seats. Food was plentiful. It was all very festive. When Sam Lewis flew in with a Constellation and saw so many people on the tarmac, he was worried that their true motive had been discovered. Then he realized that a celebration was taking place. He made a speech, saying, "It's a new era for the people of Panama." People threw their hats in the air in excitement. Excerpts of the event even made it into the New York Herald Tribune. The new Constellation which had been converted into a passenger plane at my facility in Burbank, was christened "the Pride of Panama."

For show, a plane took a presidential candidate, a group of tourists, and a cargo of Pepsi-Cola up for a flight. Then eight planes, filled to capacity, put on an air show, and flew off in formation, never to be seen again. After months of aggravation, problems with some of the engines that proved unreliable, dealing with customs officials, and bureaucratic paperwork, the planes were on their way. Time and again the crates had been checked for markings, and other proof that they were being flown out legally. The flight over the Amazon was hazardous, but the planes nevertheless reached their destination. The Jews in Palestine were beginning to get the shipments that they so desperately needed. The runway at the so-called airport in northern Tel-Aviv was lit by tin cans filled with sand and burning oil. Everything else was just as primitive, including the single shabby hangar.

When the planes arrived in Brazil three days later, a journalist figured out that the flights were actually connected to the war in Palestine. Immediately, the headlines in the papers said, "Panamanian Fliers Vanguard of Zionist Air Force." The article said it was presumed that the LAPSA airmen were Zionist volunteers transporting war materials to Palestine. Trying to dispute the story, the Brazilians were told that the fact that Jews were on the planes only proved the democratic greatness of Panama and its newly formed airline and had nothing to do with the Middle East. Nobody believed it. When the news reached Panama, both Bellefond and I were notified that the mob was after him. He and I had to get out of Panama as soon as possible.

We took the first flight out back to New York. I returned under the name of Mr. Ervin Johnson, with the intention to resume the final negotiations with the Mexican military attaché about the financial details. But just as I was leaving my hotel room to attend a meeting, a friendly bellboy informed me that the Feds were on their way up in the elevator to apprehend me. With only my briefcase and wallet, I flew out the window, down 10 flights of stairs along the fire escape, and hailed a cab. I went to a friend, Helen McLennan, a former Rockette at Radio City Music Hall. She went to Bernstein's office to give him a message from me. Then, with a forged Canadian passport provided by Teddy and money from Bernstein, I was escorted by two Haganah men across the Canadian border.

On May 14, 1948, one week after I left Panama, Steve Schwartz joined me in Canada, and we flew to Geneva. Jewish students in Geneva had organized into a group of Haganah supporters. Steve and I showed up on the doorstep of a woman whose address we were given. She recalls seeing these two Americans in cowboy boots, sitting in her living room with their legs on the cocktail table. That was her first impression of me. I told her all about what we had been doing and why we were there. I was despondent. I hated fleeing the country I love like an outlaw. Even more, I regretted the mishaps, deceptions, tragedies, confiscations, and loss of lives, and all that had thwarted plan after plan in our efforts to save another country, a country that was mine too. I felt very uncomfortable with the way we handled the LAPSA project. I wasn't proud of this deception, but we desperately needed to get the cargo out of the United States and through Panama, by whatever means. We saw an opportunity, and we took it.

That was on the date of the Declaration of Independence of the State of Israel. From Geneva, we took the train to Rome, where Danny Agronsky awaited us. He came with a mixed bag of news. The Egyptians had been bombing Tel-Aviv; 41 people were killed. Canadian volunteer George Buerling, ferrying a plane to Israel, crashed on takeoff and perished.

Our pilots were scattered in a number of places on their way to Palestine: Catania, Sicily, Dakar, French Morocco, and Casablanca.

13
MACHAL VOLUNTEERS FOR ISRAEL

More and more MACHAL volunteers streamed into Palestine to help the Jews in their fight for their homeland. They came before the War of Independence, and many stayed on to build the country after the war was over. Some were mercenaries, some could not find employment in the United States, some weren't Jewish; they came from the United States, South Africa, Australia, and other countries; they were all patriots who believed in the cause, the right of the Jewish people to live in freedom in their own country. There were mechanics, nurses and doctors, engineers, and a whole range of other professionals. They trained Israeli pilots. They helped in any way they could. They were the core of the future Israeli Air Force, and impacted the economy and security of the country. Many made Israel their home.

With the Feds on our heels and the CIA in our hair, it hadn't been simple to do what we needed to do. It wasn't all about smuggling. Working in close cooperation with Haganah, we legally bought planes for other countries and directed them to various destinations. On the way, they veered course, either directly or via Czechoslovakia, and sneaked in through the British blockade into Palestine. I heard of one valuable plane, which fell into Jewish hands purely by accident. A drug-smuggling Egyptian crashed his plane in the Negev desert. The plane was salvaged, laden with a huge amount of hashish, which the pilot dumped into the sand.

Among the planes we sent before and during the war of independence were 10 Curtis Commando C-46's through Chechoslovakia, three large Lockheed C-069 Constellations, and four B-17 Flying Fortresses, which were the main American bombers during World War II. The B-17s strafed Cairo on their way to Palestine.

While all this was going on, other challenges and activities kept us busy.

14

CODE NAME "ZEBRA"

There were rumors that the Czech arms and planes were up for grabs in Czechoslovakia. The Czech arms industry was one of the best in Europe. The Skoda Works made artillery and tanks. BRNO, a renowned fire arms manufacturer, produced rifles and machine guns. The Germans flew Messerschmidt planes during World War II that were built in Czechoslovakia by Skoda (some speculate that the Germans may have moved production to this locale in order to avoid having their facilities destroyed by the enemy during the war). The production line continued even after the war, and the stockpile that accumulated was looking for buyers. Czech pilots nicknamed the Messerschmidts "mezek" or mule. The plane was cumbersome, unpredictable, and underpowered. The Czechs were eager to get rid of them.

The surplus planes and equipment were available to all, including the Arabs — all except the Palestinian Jews. We needed them. Ben-Gurion received a coded message "Zebra" from Europe that now Czechoslovakia was willing to sell arms to Israel because this highly skilled little country was still trying to maintain its independence as a westernized democracy, though its fulcrum had shifted east. Zebra was the name of the former Luftwaffe airbase, near the town of Zatec, a little town, with one airstrip, a ribbon seen from the air, set in the midst of vast green fields[1].

---

1. In years to come, the musical "Yentl" with Barbara Streisand was filmed in Zatec.

Ben-Gurion chanced to talk to Michael Felix, a Czech-born engineer who told Ben-Gurion that his brother Otto, a lawyer, had discovered during a recent trip to Czechoslovakia that many of his old friends were now holding important official positions. Some were even in the Ministry of Defense, some of them generals. Otto Felix made the connection between the Jews and the Czechs, but the problem was how to circumvent the British blockade. The answer was to use the surplus planes that we bought, modified, and legally flown out of the United States. George Lichter, U.S. Air Force training command, was charged with preparing the pilots in Zebra to fly the Messerschmidts. He set up a program, and the American Jewish pilots who flew the planes trained the first Israeli cadets. Two Israeli pilots who had been trained by the British Royal Air Force (RAF), Ezer Weizman and Mody Alon, were sent to Czechoslovakia to train to fly the Messerschmidts for $10,000 a course.

They were driven to an air base near the Austrian border, the dreary little town of Zatek. The main square had been renamed Adolf Hitlerplatz during the German occupation. This was our Zebra operation. Our liaison with the Czech authorities was a pleasant middle-aged Czech Jew, a Holocaust survivor named Levy.

One morning, Ezer and Mody were flown to another base outside Ceske Budejovice. Their instructors were English-speaking Czechs who had served with RAF. Our pilots were handed German flight overalls, boots, parachutes, and Luftwaffe flight jackets. They were led to a two-seat trainer Ar-96A, which they would have to master before being allowed into a Messerschmidt.

Destined for various European airports, the huge Dumbos and Constellations we had acquired veered off course into Czechoslovakia. Crates of dismantled Messerschmidts, with fuselages in one plane, the rest in another, crammed with whatever engines, Czech Mauser rifles, machine guns, and ammunition we had, were sent off to Palestine. Whether sabotaged (as the rumors went) or merely hastily and faultily constructed, some of the planes were inoperable. At Zebra, there was even a Connie with a LAPSA C-46 with its Panamanian blue registration number RX-138 waiting for Messerschmidst to be dismantled. Our mechanics, flown in by Raab, prepared the planes, stacking crates of ammunition, and fueling up.

Several more of our pilots had been on a crash course familiarizing themselves with the Messerschmidts. Our pilots completed 95 airlifts between Czechoslovakia and Palestine.

The swastika was removed and replaced with the Star of David. The irony of a German Messerschmit, produced in Czechoslovakia, flown by American Jewish pilots fighting for the creation and protection of the Jewish state wasn't lost on anyone. The problem was that Poland and Romania did not permit Czech planes to cross their airspace. The only roundabout way they managed to fly was through Yugoslavia. Meanwhile, the Jews were waiting, and waiting, and waiting at an abandoned British airfield. After 12 hours of nonstop flight, the C-46's were unloaded, refueled from hand pumps by men with flashlights, back in the air in an hour and a half with a different crew.

Young men in the Haganah, who had served with allied air forces during the war, planned the airborne supply operation. We flew high over Austrian and Italian mountains via Corsica in far from luxurious conditions — no oxygen, erratic heaters, and box lunches. In Corsica, we denied carrying firearms and any military equipment, showed the major the crates marked "glass — fragile," transacted business, and refueled at 10 cents per gallon. We were off again with very poor radio communication, relying mainly on the navigator's skill and experience, flying at night under the radar, unseen and unacknowledged, using radio signals over unfriendly territories whenever necessary.

We landed on secretly built well-camouflaged air strips in Palestine by being in secret contact at regular intervals with the airfield Aquir at the final leg of the flight. The operation was called Yakum Purkan, meaning salvation would be coming from the skies. I watched with pride and emotion as the Messerschmidts with the Star of David spilled out the treasures that we had so impatiently and desperately waited for. I knew that within 24 hours they would be assembled and ready for action. The C-46's with a different crew flew back to Zebra to pick up more Messerschmidts, ammunition, and guns.

Back and forth our pilots flew, frantically smuggling planes out and smuggling planes in. Every flight was a risk. Every cargo delivered was a jubilation. Every plane that was damaged was a friend lost, mourned by me and the rest of the crew. I once saw Leo sitting forlorn at the side of a crashed plane, as though at the graveside of a dear one. I knew exactly how he felt.

One C-46 that returned to Zatec was grounded by the American authorities, who thought that it had been smuggling weapons to the Italian communists.

15

THE INDEPENDENCE OF ISRAEL

On May 14, 1948, in the opera house in Tel-Aviv, David Ben-Gurion declared the independence of the State of Israel. I was proud that America was the first country to recognize Israel's sovereignty and saw the irony that they did so, and yet the embargo against supplying arms to Israel to defend itself was still in effect.

The celebrations in the street were overwhelming. After 2,000 years, the Jews finally had their own home. People were dancing and cheering and celebrating. Ben-Gurion faced the day with foreboding. He anticipated the inevitable war with dread.

On the following day, at dawn of May 15, 1948, Israel was viciously attacked by six Arab countries: Egypt, Lebanon, Syria, Transjordan, Saudi Arabia, and Iraq. The most serious enemy was Egypt. The War of Independence began. Greatly outnumbered, with very little military equipment, the Israelis relied on heroism, ingenuity, grit, and the help of American volunteers.

The Egyptian column of some 300 armored vehicles was pitched against the first four clumsy, refurbished Messerschmidts armed with guns that we had sent the Israeli Air Force. The Egyptians were stunned, shocked, and completely discombobulated; it effectively halted the advance.

I was appointed Deputy Commander of the Israel Air Force, with the rank of Lieutenant Colonel, in charge of technical services. I accepted the nomination as long as I was acknowledged as a civilian; no oath of allegiance, no uniform. My duties were, essentially, to keep the fighters, bombers, and transport planes flying. Our unit was named American Transport Company (ATC). Sam Lewis and Hal Auerbach were ATC's commanders but considered themselves answerable to me. The Israeli Air Force played a tremendous part in the fight for independence. They frequently strafed the enemy armored columns and troop concentrations unopposed. The Connies continued to fly non-stop from Zebra to Israel.

Accidents happened. Planes and lives were lost. Our highly skilled pilots did their utmost, but sometimes that wasn't enough. Sometimes our luck ran out. One of our Connies returned to Zebra for repair after crashing. All the passengers were shaken but safe. I saw Sam Lewis sitting by the damaged plane and could tell from his dejected posture that he was thinking as I was thinking: every plane we had sent from the States was such an effort, such a big deal, and to lose one of them was like losing a friend.

In Washington, President Truman received a secret communique from CIA Director Roscoe Hillenkoetter about a clandestine air transport operation that defied the neutrality act and export control law by sending surplus war material to Israel through Czechoslovakia.

Bending to American pressure, the Czech government ordered us out of Zebra. It was forced to close the airport to LAPSA flights. Within 72 hours, the base was to be evacuated, all equipment and personnel out. I flew to Zebra. Ernie Stehlik wanted to remain to continue repairing the damaged Connie, otherwise it would have to be left behind. I agreed. Raab remained with Ernie to fly the repaired C-54 to Israel. George Lichter, Israeli cadet, smuggled his Czech girlfriend out in mechanic's overalls. The last flight from Zebra was truly hazardous. First one engine gave out, then the second one. On two engines, Larry landed in shallow waters close enough to safety, wet but unharmed. The C-49 was salvageable.

Though officially closed, the Czechs were eager to continue their relationship with us. They were phasing out their operations and were anxious to dispose of their Messerschmidts and spare parts. So now and then we continued to pick up what we needed. We also negotiated with them for their Spitfires, which we badly wanted. They agreed to sell us 40 Spitfires. In groups of five or six, they flew to Israel. The operation, called "Velveta," flew via Yugoslavia.

Another tragedy, another loss. One of the Spitfires crashed into a mountain in Montenegro, killing Sam Pomerantz, the mechanical genius who figured out how to create a fuel system that made it possible to fly non-stop to Israel.

Closing down Zebra, our C-46's took on the next project to take Eilat, situated at the southernmost tip of the barren Negev desert, on the shore of the Red Sea. The ancient city of Eilat had become desolate. It consisted of two bare little mud huts, a tiny nautical museum, and a few scraggly bushes of red flowers trying bravely to survive in the arid land. By sharp contrast, a world of exquisite corals and colorful fish lived in the super clear blue sea.

There was one road that led through the desert from Eilat to the biblical city of Beersheba. Beersheba was at the northern end of the desert. There was nothing but desert between the two cities.

The borders of Egypt, Jordan, Saudi Arabia, and Israel converge at Eilat, at the northern point of the long Red Sea.

This Negev desert is two-thirds of the entire area allotted to Israel by the UN. Whoever owned Eilat owned the Negev.

The Egyptian army was pushing into the Negev, which would split the entire country in two. They controlled the only road from Eilat to the Beersheva.

The chief of the Israeli army was General Yigal Yadin, a renowned archeologist. Through his archeological studies, he knew that there had once been an ancient road through the Negev. His solution was to circumvent the main road and lead the Israeli army along the ancient biblical road covered by deep sand all the way south to Eilat, taking the Egyptian army totally by surprise. There was no one there to protect it. We took Eliat.

Most certainly a matter of the right person in the right position at the right time.

Parallel to that, our American pilots and ATC crew were handed a job. There were no airstrips in the Negev. I sent Leo Gardner to find an appropriate spot to create them. Two strips created for C-46 landing, appropriately named "Dustbowl One" and Dustbowl Two" by our pilots, connected Eilat to the rest of Israel. Flying dusk to dawn, flight time 30 minutes each way, with Stars of David and Israel Air Force numbers instead of the Panamanian markings, our planes carried soldiers, guns, ammunition, medication, and food over the desert.

In the largest aerial offensive of the war, 13 bombers took to the air. Actually, only three B-17s were bombers. The others, carriers, C-47 Dakotas and C-46, improvised. Bombs attached to the cabin floors in metal trays were released one bomb at a time, and kicked out the open cabin door. It worked. Eilat was ours. We owned the desert.

Jerusalem was besieged. The battle for control of the city was ferocious. According to the partition plan, the city was supposed to be placed under international rule, but neither the Israelis nor the Arabs agreed. The main road to west Jerusalem, where the majority of the Jewish population lived, was blockaded by the Arabs to prevent supplies from being brought in. Our soldiers launched attacks to break through the blockades and built a secret alternate road leading to the city before the truce was enforced. But Jerusalem was split between us and the Jordanians; east Jerusalem, including the Old City and the Jewish holy sites, was in Jordanian hands, and west Jerusalem, where the majority of Jews lived, was ours.

While the fight for independence was raging, immigrants were being brought in, largely survivors of the Holocaust. Many of the untrained young people were immediately drafted into the military. Mody Alon, one of our only two Israeli pilots, was killed in a Messerschmidt landing accident. Another somber occasion, another devastating loss. At times it seemed that what we were trying to do was doomed, but we persisted; we felt we had no choice. The world stood by, passive and indifferent. Our casualties were heavy. Inch by inch, we defended our land.

We bombed Damascus, Gaza, Majdal, and Faluja. After four days of around the clock strafing, the Egyptians were finally convinced that there was no way they could win this war. On October 15th, the United Nations ordered a ceasefire. But skirmishes continued, and the ceasefire went ignored by the Arabs.

Eventually, brokered by the United Nations, Egypt signed an armistice agreement on February 24, 1949. Lebanon, Jordan, and Syria signed separate agreements by June 1949. The lines were drawn. Borders were adjusted. The war of independence was over. As someone pointed out to the Israeli public, "Al Schwimmer had done it. He had smuggled an air force to Israel." And that won the war.

The British Royal Air Force still contested our aerial supremacy. In early January 1949, five RAF Spitfires infringed on our air space. The Israeli Spitfires intercepted them and shot them all down. That was the last British aerial incursion into Israel.

We had been negotiating for a long time with the Mexican government about acquiring their P-47's, and as soon as the money changed hands, the planes would be ours. But the Israeli government told me to cancel the deal because, without even consulting with me or even the courtesy of asking for my opinion, they decided to purchase 25 Messerschmidts from Czechoslovakia instead and couldn't back out of their contract. That upset me very much. I felt that the P-47's were superior to the watered-down S-199's. They were clumsy, and I felt they were settling for the worst plane simply because someone had decided it was to be. And our pilots were not familiar with these planes. Many logistics decisions made no sense to me, including disassembling the planes, loading them on to our C-46's, and flying them to wherever they could be refueled for the long trip to Israel. And of course, a lot of money had to change hands, money collected largely from donations. Disappointments, betrayals, disasters, and successes were all part of creating the air force.

The Knesset formally elected David Ben-Gurion prime minister and minister of defense.

Immediately after the war, the process of rebuilding the country began. 350,000 immigrants were flown in, predominantly from Eastern Europe, largely the destitute survivors of the Holocaust. The influx of immigrants had to be absorbed. Most of the immigrants didn't know Hebrew, and many had no skills and very little education. They streamed in from everywhere, bringing a diversity of cultures and languages, speaking Arabic, Russian, German, French, Romanian, Farsi, Hungarian, Turkish, Ladino, Polish, and other languages. Most of them had to learn Hebrew. In the first two years, the population tripled. Immigrant camps sprouted all over the country. How does one cope with the enormity of dealing with this absorption? There was no precedent. It would have been an impossible task for even a rich country to absorb such an influx. Shortage of food, housing, and jobs had to be dealt with. Food was rationed during this period of austerity. Among the volunteers who stayed on to participate in the creation of the Israeli Air Force were many of my friends, including the best pilots, Sam Lewis and Leo Gardner. They undoubtedly enabled the illustrious Israeli Air Force to become what it is today. During the war, and beyond, I served as chief engineer of the air force. In that capacity, I had the privilege of meeting many important figures who shaped the new government. I formed a special relationship with David Ben-Gurion, the first Prime Minister of Israel.

There was a need for a national airline, Ben-Gurion insisted. I was proud that the first captains of the Israeli Airline, EL AL, were the ATC pilots. The first planes we chose were the old LAPSA C-54 and Boeings, which we painted, carpeted, and furnished with seats to create a fleet. The name chosen, El Al, is a combination of words: EL meaning to or towards, AL means up, above, (sky). A witty Israeli came up with a pun. EL in Hebrew is also one of the names for God. AL, he decided, was meant for me. My Hebrew wasn't good enough to comprehend it at first and that certainly wasn't the interpretation that I had in mind. The C-54 miraculously transformed into an elegant passenger plane, with the official logo of El Al and registration numbers in place, brought the former U.S. Treasury Secretary Henry Morgenthau for a state visit. Dr. Chaim Weizmann, the first President of the State of Israel was also brought in by El Al.

16
FREE BUT UNEMPLOYABLE

Shortly after the Israeli War of Independence was over, in early September, I got a subpoena to return to the United States to face trial for the crime of violating the Neutrality Act and Export Control Law. I was indicted on September 30, 1949. I remained in the United States until the trial was over. Then, in May 1953, we were found guilty, fined, but not incarcerated, free to rebuild our lives. But we were unemployable. No airline would hire us. I couldn't find a job with any of the aircraft companies because my civil rights had been revoked and I was not allowed to be employed in any official capacity. We had no right to hold a government position, vote, or receive veteran benefits.

Five months after the trial was over, Hank Greenspun was indicted again, this time for his part in the Idalia incident. The government's star witness, the owner of the yacht Idalia, the "patriotic Jew," certainly told the truth when he testified that he had transported the military equipment to Acapulco only because Hank had held a pistol to his temple. Hank was found guilty but would have no incarceration, only a stiff fine that the Israeli government paid.

The United States was still reeling from its economic crisis. Unemployment was high, and there were some added problems: the relationship with the Soviet Union and the distrust of communism during the McCarthy era. This ally in the war against the Nazis had suddenly become the biggest threat to U.S. security. In addition, the embargo on arms and military equipment to Israel had not been lifted. We were suspected of dealing with the Soviet Union, no proof needed.

I bought an old Cadillac convertible and went to California with a small group of friends who were in the same predicament. I borrowed money, we pooled our resources, and we raised the seed money to create our own business and help Israel's El Al airline keep its planes flying. Again, I set up an aircraft servicing company in a glorified garage at Lockheed Terminal in Burbank, named Intercontinental Airline. There were nine of us in the beginning. Nobody cared about criminal records in the aircraft repair business, as long as we got the job done. On my desk I had a small plastic replica of a LAPSA plane, a souvenir from Panama. Most of my employees were friends who had helped me with the smuggling operation.

We rented a sprawling ranch house with a pool on North Vine Street and the nine of us bachelors lived in luxury in a "commune." We even had a cook. Many of our former volunteers came to hang out and reminisce about our escapades. 26-year-old Shimon Peres came to Burbank on his honeymoon, and I lent him my Cadillac to show his bride around. We worked, we danced with girlfriends, and, repairing airplanes for a few steady customers, we managed to make a living, though not a luxurious one. Bob Prescott, who had started the Flying Tiger Airline, sent us his C-46 planes to service. We sub-contracted for Lockheed. But our main aim was to continue helping Israel by repairing the planes we continued to send them.

Shimon and I worked on a deal to acquire 30 surplus Mustang fighters for the Israeli Air Force, but the U.S. military decided to scrap them instead. They clipped off the wings and cut the fuselage into two. A junk dealer in Texas bought the scrap and sold it to me at cost. Our mechanics disassembled the planes, put them together like a jigsaw puzzle, dismantled them again, packed them into crates labeled "irrigation equipment," and shipped them to Israel. These were just some of the ways we managed to help Israel acquire much-needed aircraft.

EL AL Israeli airline contracted us to refurbish and modify two Connies that had been released from U.S. impound to its rightful owner, the Israeli government. The third Connie would be released from Czechoslovakia and fly to the United States for repair. We provided the Israeli Air Force with several squadrons of P-51's. We acquired Mustangs and maintained them for the Israeli Air Force in its formative years.

The Israeli Air Force acquired a World War II Mosquito fighter-bomber, which we repaired. Our pilot, Ray Kurtz, convinced me that he could fly it to Israel. He stopped to refuel at a United States Air Force base in Greenland, took off, and was never seen again. We notified Shimon Peres, and he came immediately from Israel to join the search party. Steve Schwartz flew us, with Ray's wife Ruth aboard. We tried desperately to find the plane and hoped that Ray had survived. For days we flew over the blinding snow, touching down near Eskimo villages to ask whether anyone had seen an airplane crash. Sadly, his body was never recovered. His widow never forgave me, nor I myself. The search itself was hazardous — we flew over the mountains, almost ran out of fuel, and landed the huge Constellation like a lousy glider. Many years later, the frozen remains of Ray Kurtz were found in the mountains in Canada.

Business was good. We expanded and had close to 100 people on our payroll, and more work than we could handle.

We continued obtaining planes for the Israeli Air Force. They needed P-51 fighters to replace the ancient Spitfires, and though the U.S. government wasn't selling them, preferring to scrap them for metal, we managed to acquire the destroyed fuselages, and cut off wings and other bits and pieces that were sold to dealers throughout the country, that were transported to us. Thirty rebuilt planes were legally placed aboard ships and sent to Israel. We repaired El Al and Israeli Air Force planes almost at cost. Other damaged planes came to us in Burbank. We repaired them and sent them to Israel. We found a solution for hazardous and difficult situations. We went to Czechoslovakia to pick up Connies, repaired and modified them, and sent them to Israel as well.

One day, a black limo with an entourage of security cars pulled up in front of the workshop in my corner of the airport. Through the tinted window, I saw an unmistakable mane of bushy white hair. Out came David Ben-Gurion, his assistant Shimon Peres, and Teddy Kollek. They had been on a fundraising mission and were invited to see President Truman at the White House. Ben-Gurion had asked Peres, "Isn't Al Schwimmer in the States?" Peres said that yes, I was in Burbank, California. Ben Gurion took Peres with him to see me. First, he asked whether I'd learned Hebrew by now. Then he asked me what I was doing there, and I said, "making a living." He said I should be in Israel, setting up a facility for repairing airplanes (which the Jews barely had at that time). I realized he was right; Israel needed to be independent and strong, and air supremacy was vital. Israel needed an aircraft industry. Israel needed me. I walked him through our facility, to show him how we did things: the C-46 we were modifying for EL AL, the engines we were overhauling for the IAF. Again he said that we needed to have an aviation industry in Israel. He kept harping at me. He told me I was "the right man in the wrong place." He wanted me in the right place. That coincided with my view that Israel had to be independent and self-sufficient, not to rely upon the whims of foreign countries for its survival.

I had two stipulations: no politics involved, and I would do things my way. I knew that I myself would bear the responsibility. The challenge intrigued me, and I was ready to take it on. I would run it the way I knew how — the American way.

I handed my company and hangar over to my partners, which they liquidated two years later. I moved back to Israel.

17

BEDEK AVIATION

Ben-Gurion knew that in order to survive, Israel must become an industrial power. And that wasn't part of my earliest dream to build airplanes?

None of the other members of the Israeli cabinet could understand the need for an aircraft industry. When we went to the Knesset and told the cabinet that we planned to set up an aircraft company, the ministers scoffed. They burst out laughing. "You want to build airplanes? You don't even know how to build bicycles. Whatever we need, we can buy from America!" This wasn't strictly true, as they weren't selling us anything because the embargo was still enforced. With Egyptian guns aiming at the Tel-Aviv skyline and Syrian guns pointing down from the Golan Heights at the Sea of Galilee, Israel was vulnerable.

It seemed that none of the other ministers realized that. None of them wanted the responsibility of dealing with this scatterbrain idea. Not the minister of finance and industry, not the minister of transportation, and not General Moshe Dayan. But Ben-Gurion's vision coincided with mine. We must be self-sufficient, independent. He was prime minister and minister of defense. He said the plant would be under the jurisdiction of the ministry of defense. He delegated the direct contact to his assistant, Shimon Peres, who also believed wholeheartedly in the importance of the company. Ben-Gurion lived by the philosophy that if an advisor said something was impossible, it was time to fire the advisor. I liked his way of thinking. Young Peres was an advisor whom Ben-Gurion never had to fire.

Our goal was to create a homeland that did not depend upon handouts from the Americans or anyone else and could not be threatened by embargos. Combining intelligence, guts, and good management, we could become a modern industrial success story. Land-locked in the Middle East, midway between Asia and Europe, we could create a maintenance and repair facility for international air traffic. We could overhaul commercial and military planes and sell them on the world market to countries that couldn't afford new planes, and service planes flying between Asia and Europe. It would create jobs for the Israelis, bring in hard currency, and boost the economy. Eventually we could turn to manufacturing as well, even jet fighter planes to make the Israeli Air Force a powerful deterrent to whoever tried to destroy us. Why not? Big dreams. Ambitious dreams. With a team that included Ben-Gurion, Peres, and me, we could do it.

Getting money for our project entailed a great deal of arm-twisting by Ben-Gurion, until even the finance minister, who had originally had misgivings about the feasibility of our plans, eventually became our staunchest supporter.

In 1952, bulldozers cleared the nettles and thorns in an area near the Lod airport and started preparations for the aircraft company. I set up shop in a large shed-like building next to the airport, in terrain as desolate as the moonscape. One of the skills I had developed during my smuggling period was improvising to get things done the impossible way.

We started out with a Quonset hut, an outhouse, and plans for a number of hangars and shops. In the sand and gravel, construction equipment and scaffolding proclaimed loudly the beginning of an aircraft company. Meanwhile, we turned a dilapidated structure into a hangar. The bottom floor was the workshop and the top floor was for the offices. It resembled a chaotic junkyard, with piles of dismembered surplus planes and crates crammed with spare parts everywhere. We were short even the basic tools, like crowbars.

My projection was that within 18 months, we would employ 800 people. Later we would have an office building and a dining room, not that anyone in the government believed that. The press was as skeptical as the ministers. Ben-Gurion withstood all the political and internal wrangling and encouraged the construction of the plant, despite the financial difficulties the country was wrapped up in. By then, Shimon Peres was appointed director-general of the Ministry of Defense.

Hyman Shamir and Danny Agronsky joined me in creating the dream. We hired several experts from the U.S. We called it Bedek, a term with biblical connotations that was somehow connected with an ancient Hebrew inscription on a stone in a Judean temple in the ninth century B.C. It referred in some way to restoration. It was a short, catchy name, easily pronounced in any language.

Bedek Aviation was officially inaugurated in 1953, two years after its conception. David Ben-Gurion, Shimon Perez, members of the cabinet, the administration of Bedek, and most of the employees attended this significant event. A large billboard proclaimed our presence, visible from the main highway.

I was president. Hyman Shamir was vice-president. We hired professional engineers, technicians, mechanics, and pilots, mostly from abroad but there were some experienced Israelis as well. We hired retired officers from the Israeli Air Force who had been trained in aircraft maintenance and overhaul in Spartan School of Aeronautics in Tulsa, Oklahoma. We hired Israelis and new immigrants from many countries with various levels of technical skill and experience, and many with no technical skills whatsoever. Most of them didn't know Hebrew. They spoke Romanian, Polish, Arabic, French, German, Hungarian, Turkish, and other languages. Many had numbers on their forearms tattooed by the Nazis in the concentration camps. Language and cultural barriers had to be overcome. We created training programs. Our main focus was to service, maintain, and overhaul planes for the Israeli Air Force, and they remained our main customer. We also worked with the Israeli airline El Al. Many of the pilots who flew El Al were the ones I recruited for our smuggling operations. Within a year we had all of 500 employees, quite a large company by Israeli standards. Gradually, self-doubt evolved into confidence, into the belief that we could do it. Gradually our experience grew, so did our reputation. Worldwide. We were knowledgeable, trustworthy, and reasonable. We began to repair airplanes from many different countries.

18

"ON WINGS OF EAGLES"

The Yemenite Muslim government responded to the establishment of Israel with anti-Jewish riots and mob violence. The Jews had lived in Yemen for many centuries. The poorest Jewish citizens still lived by their faith, had synagogues and schools, and kept their traditions. Now they were persecuted even further, were burned and tortured. Ben-Gurion was bent on gathering the Jewish exiles and made the decision to save these Yemenite Jews and bring them to Israel, so we planned a secret airlift. Shortly after, in May 1949, the Imam of Yemen suddenly, and unexpectedly, agreed to let the Jewish people leave. Almost 49,000 Jews crossed 1,600 miles of hostile territory to temporary transit camps in Aden. They were to be airlifted in an operation officially called "On Wings of Eagles" that was colloquially known as Operation Magic Carpet. The American Jewish Distribution Committee (JDC), a humanitarian organization, funded it. Working out a deal with Alaska Airlines, Leo Gardner and Sam Lewis were among the pilots who flew back and forth. These were simple people, totally unfamiliar with airplanes and skeptical of those metal objects that they were supposed to board. It took some convincing before they believed that their prayers were answered and that, according to the Bible, they were being brought to the Holy Land "On the wings of eagles." I also hired Bob Prescott's Flying Tigers for this mission. To the horror and disbelief of the crew, the passengers tried to sit in the aisles and turn on their burners to cook their food. When the refugees landed, they kissed the ground. It was a most moving scene. It took 16 months, about 380 flights, and countless hazardous experiences, with the pilots pushing the aircraft to the limits, to complete this unique mission.

We also hired Bob Prescott's Flying Tigers to bring in more than 13,000 Jews from Iraq in "Operation Ali Baba." The Jewish communities had existed in these countries for centuries but were no longer welcome there.

Operation "Beta Israel," beginning in 1977, airlifted 22,000 Jews from Ethiopia by El Al. Other airlifts brought in Jews from Sudan in 1979 and Addis Ababa in 1990.

So, El Al, which started as a division of ATC, which had once been LAPSA, which came from Service Airways, all began with Schwimmer Aviation in Burbank, California.

19

MEETING RINA

One evening in 1954, I was invited to a party, to which I reluctantly went, even though the party was in honor of Charlie Winters (the non-Jew who had sold us B-17's and the only one who went to jail). It was his first visit in Israel, and many of my Machal buddies would be there. The evening before, we had all been celebrating my birthday on the Tel-Aviv beach. The next day, Tuxy Blau, a South African volunteer, brought a girl to the party. Her name was Rina. I was charmed. We chatted. I called her the next day and said, "I'll buy you dinner." She didn't understand this American way of inviting a girl out. I didn't understand the sensitive issue of food during the time of austerity and rationing in Israel and was amazed at her reaction.

"Do I look hungry?" she asked.

I took her out anyway. I was in love. She was the first (and only, it turned out) Jewish girl I ever dated. When she came to Bridgeport to meet my family, my mother was ecstatic. Not only was she pretty, intelligent, and delightful, she was Jewish! They hit it off. How could they not? Rina's father, though, was suspicious of me from the start. He said to Rina, he was sure I was holding something back. I must be married, have a wife and a few children somewhere in America. He had to protect his little girl. Within a short time we became the best of friends.

On January 29, 1955 we got married in London. I came from Connecticut after my mother's "Yortseit," the annual memorial service, and made all the bureaucratic arrangements for the wedding. Again, my German-sounding name was under suspicion by the rabbi. I had to send a wire to my friend in Jerusalem to get a copy of the confirmation that I was indeed Jewish. Tuxie Blau stood at the gate of the synagogue and managed to recruit 10 people to witness our ceremony, according to Jewish tradition. Sam Lewis was my best man, and his wife, Jean, was Rina's maid of honor. After the ceremony, I called my family in Bridgeport to tell them that I got married. The honeymoon bordered on fiasco and would have been a problem if not for Rina's understanding. Just as we checked into the hotel in Toromeno, Sicily, I was informed that there were a number of messages from Israel. I called Peres and was told that I need to go back to Israel immediately. There was a crisis. What could be that important that I had to cut my honeymoon short? I told Rina, and she burst out crying. I tried to comfort her and said she could stay on if she wanted to. Wrong thing to say!

"All by myself? On our honeymoon? That's even worse!" she exclaimed.

She returned to Israel with me. That set the tone and the priorities in our married life. It had to be the way it was; the price she had to pay for being married to a man with a dream.

20
BEDEK CONTINUES TO EXPAND

Shortly after we were married, Ben-Gurion negotiated a $1 million deal with Prime Minister U Nu of Burma to purchase 34 Spitfires, which the Israeli Air Force was no longer using, along with a large number of rifles. We serviced the planes, painted them with the colors of the Burmese Air Force, along with their logo, and they were ready to go. It wasn't that simple. Nothing seems to ever be. Flying over Arab countries would have been dangerous, so I asked Leo Gardner to transport them through England. I called him early in the morning. He was glad to do it, but asked, "Can I have a cup of coffee first?" Within two days he was in England, where he hired pilots for the long trek. They overcame emergency landings and fuel problems as they flew in groups of three. One of the ace pilots was a petite 5-foot woman.

1955 was a milestone in the growth of Bedek. Barely a year after we set up shop, we received the FAA and United States CAA certification, and approval to service American military and civilian aircraft. We then received a similar certification from the Air Registration Board of Great Britain. We were licensed to repair, maintain, and service international planes. We began to work with foreign countries. We successfully participated in a program called "Zero Defects," effectively increasing our efficiency. We were internationally recognized as the most adaptable repair and service center in the industry. We signed contracts to work on engines by manufacturers such as General Electric, Pratt & Whitney, Rolls Royce, and Hispana-Suisa. And gradually, even planes from as far away as Asia began to land in Lod airport for repair.

Our customers included Lanchile, Air Peru, Air Mexico, Iran Air, Guyana Airline, Air France, Lot Polish airline, Uganda Air Force and more. Iran was one of our most important customers. We were secretly helped sometimes, from totally unexpected sources, to out bid our competitors for contracts for repair jobs. Our most important customer still was the IAF.

I commuted between Israel, the U.S., and Europe, procuring materials, tools, and once even a complete maintenance depot. We added more hangars and shops.

But suddenly it seemed that everything collapsed around me. The director of El Al didn't need our services anymore, and neither did the air force.

Overnight, Bedek appeared to be "a drain on the economy." It became apparent that the criticism wasn't directed at Bedek, but at me personally. I was seen as an "irresponsible careerist," an American opportunist, and such. Dan Tolkowsky, air force commander, in particular, saw me either as a rival or a threat, certainly an outsider. Ben-Gurion was unwaveringly on my side. I was confused and surprised since Bedek was becoming the industry supporting the defense of Israel. I eventually saw the real picture: Bedek was an extension of Ben-Gurion's domain, and the attack was vicariously on him. My success was his success and not popular with the opposition party. Shimon Peres was not surprised. Ben-Gurion told me that it's all right, and to just keep going. Shortly after, both the air force and El Al returned to work with us.

We created permanent buildings for engine overhaul, machine shops, aircraft electronics, test benches, hydraulics, instrumentation, radio, basic aircraft maintenance, carpentry, and inspection. I had visions of a giant industry, eventually manufacturing our own planes.

I began to seek out and recruit more people and to delegate responsibilities. The cadre of executives from abroad began to train Israelis to take over their positions.

Gradually, Bedek continued to expand. The Israeli Air Force was our major customer, but not the only one. Both the Israeli Air Force, and EL AL airline relied heavily on the technical capabilities of Bedek.

A tragic accident occurred that did not involve me directly, but deeply troubled me anyway. An EL AL plane on its way between Vienna and Tel-Aviv erroneously flew over Bulgarian airspace and was shot down, killing all 40 passengers. The fatal Constellation was our original Connie.

I was constantly on the go: meeting with heads of states, signing contracts with international aircraft companies, and developing businesses and projects. During one of my trips to the United States, when I accompanied Shimon Peres, then minister of defense, on a fundraising mission, we were invited to the White House. President George Bush Sr. shook my hand and said he was very honored to meet me. He had heard so much about me. He probably failed to recognize the guest sitting next to him at his table as the "felon" whom he was trying to capture when he was head of the CIA, the smuggler who defied the Neutrality Act and smuggled planes, engines, spare parts, and other military equipment to defend Israel in its fight for independence.

After leaving the office at the end of the day, I had a habit of stopping by the shops to talk to the workers, from managers to floor-sweepers, and drink endless cups of tea with them, try to resolve their issues or their most trivial complaints, and take an interest in their personal lives. There was never a problem with the union, and unlike many other companies in Israel, there wasn't a single strike. Asked once, what was the secret of the success of IAI, I said unequivocally, the employees.

I always had a sweet tooth, and my favorite dessert was the Viennese chocolate Sachre Torte. I treated myself to it whenever I went abroad. One day a package was delivered to me in the office. Viennese Sachre Torte! My assistant, Aryeh Orbach, told me not to touch it. He called the security officers. They took the package away, and detonated a bomb that had been meant for me. What had aroused Orbach's suspicion was that there was no sender's address. I owe my life to his vigilance. I was told that I was on the Arab hit list.

My relationship with Ezer Weizman, the Chief of Israel Air Force, was anything but amicable. What I thought was appropriate, he immediately, automatically, negated. He was set on acquiring the Hercules, at a $1,000,000 each from the United States. I wanted to buy the huge Stratocruisers, at $50,000 each, to modify them for military use, to carry jeeps, paratroopers, and tanks by putting swing doors on the planes. Ezer called these recycled junkyard planes. It had become a matter of personal prestige for him to get his way.

He showed up at my home while I was shaving and announced, "I don't want the Stratos." The government's decision to acquire them was a mistake. He said, "I don't think you know what your position here is!" My position here was president of the largest, most sophisticated company in Israel, world-renowned for repairing, maintaining, and building aircraft. He was putting me in my place! He told me that "his" air force would accept nothing but the best. He called me an idiot and then he left.

21

OPERATION MUSKETEERS

In 1957, in an act of aggression, Egyptian president Nasser closed off the Strait of Tiran in the Suez Canal, cutting off all access to foreign ships. He nationalized the Suez Canal, 40 percent of which was owned by the British. They sank all the ships that were unlucky enough to be docked in port.

In response, France and Britain, together with Israel, launched an attack on Egypt to occupy the Canal Zone. I wasn't in on all the behind-the-scene diplomacy that went on before the attack. Massive waves of bombers and fighter planes, attacked by Soviet anti-aircraft guns, hit targets all across the Sinai desert. IAI repaired our air force planes, both piston and jet. My old Dumbos dropped paratroopers into the desert, to capture Egyptian bases, and in a short time, the Egyptian soldiers scattered their arms all across the Sinai, and fled. Israeli pilots brought down a plane flying Egyptian military chiefs from Damascus to Cairo. Practically overnight, the Egyptian army collapsed. A Soviet MiG-21 was shot down in the desert, and the pilot ran for his life. For our mechanics, that was an opportunity to study the secrets of the most formidable Soviet plane: MiG. The G stood for Mikhail Gurevich, a Jewish son of a winery mechanic from a remote village. The Mi stood for Artem Mikoyan, an Armenian engineer from the Asian wastelands. The partners cranked out new more and more sophisticated models every year. Israeli forces pushed towards the Suez Canal, and Ariel Sharon took it upon himself to lead his troops across the canal, surrounding an Egyptian platoon.

The U.S. government, outraged that the plan had not been shared with them, and had not been consulted or informed of this combined attack on Egypt, intervened. They were afraid that this attack would draw the Soviet Union to the Egyptian side and demanded immediate ceasefire and complete withdrawal from the Egyptian territory. They responded with threats of such magnitude to the British economy that the British quickly withdrew from Suez. The French followed. We had no choice. This military success turned into a political fiasco. The Arabs convinced themselves that they had won the war, and that Nasser was their hero, stronger than ever.

The first United Nations peacekeeping corps was sent to the Middle East.

But most importantly, this war demonstrated that Israel would not hesitate to protect its interests and citizens and had the capability to do so. The pilots proved it. But despite its military prowess, Israel was a small nation, dependent upon the political whims of the superpowers.

Once again, it confirmed our need to manufacture our own aircraft. Bedek was ready to convert from a repair and overhaul facility to a manufacturer of airplanes and other technical ventures.

Life was following a challenging yet pleasant rhythm. Rina and I moved to Savyon, an elegant but somewhat isolated neighborhood that was close to the airport. I had a family I delighted in. Our son Danny, and later our daughter Dafna, were born. I somewhat understood that it must be difficult for Rina to spend so much time without me while I was abroad for weeks at a time. I counted on her to do a good job raising the children on her own. I felt that that's the way it had to be. Things were going smoothly with all the foreign countries that had their planes serviced with us. We worked with countries worldwide, but the Israeli Air Force was and will always be the most important client. In wartime our facility becomes officially a part of the Israeli defense forces, and that becomes top priority.

Now was the time to start planning to create our own military jets.

All the while, from the day that Israel became independent, we had to deal with frequent skirmishes along the borders with the Arab states, and deadly attacks on civilians by terrorist groups. The Egyptians used ex-Nazi experts in their propaganda, as well as plans to build missiles. Egypt was supplied the most sophisticated MiG fighters by the Soviet Union. The U.S. embargo on military equipment to the Middle East was never lifted. Israel was the only country affected by that.

In trying to restore Arab pride, Nasser had German-designed Egyptian missiles called "Al Qahar" and "Al Zafer" paraded through the streets in Cairo. The roaring crowds didn't know that the missiles were made of cardboard because the missiles' guidance systems were so poor that they tended to loop back, to boomerang the friendly troops.

22

THE FRENCH CONNECTION

For years, Shimon Peres was personally involved in establishing and developing ties with France, our first powerful friend and ally. Post-war France seemed to be principled and indomitable, and the government of Guy Mollet almost instinctively gave its support to Israel. They sold us the new Vautour fighter. When I said I felt the opposition was against us and will forget us if they were in power, he said, "No, with us it will be different. You'll see."

I was introduced to all the major figures on the French political scene. I was invited to their offices and was a welcome guest in their homes. They all pledged their support to Israel.

My dreams were becoming more of a reality. Ezer Weitzman, commander of the IAF, never believed in our capability to create our own airplane. He once pointed arrogantly at his palm and said to me, "Hair will grow on the palm of my hand before I see a plane built by Bedek that the air force can use."

In 1957, I took a team with me to Toulouse, where we discussed a deal to manufacture the Fouga, a training jet, in Bedek. The manufacturers of Fouga sold us the license, a complete package of plans, specifications, parts, machines, jigs, dies, tools, and training courses for the Bedek mechanics who would assemble them. In the immigrant camps that were sprouting all over the country, I was lucky to find some workers with modest mechanical skills, but for the most part, the others had no technical experience at all.

My team and I commuted between Israel and Toulouse, acquiring information and material. Then we modified the original plans and improved on the original designs to fit our needs. Where necessary, we manufactured entirely new parts and attached different wings. It was no longer just a training jet. We adapted it for far more stressful conditions and transformed the French training jet into an Israeli fighter plane ready for combat.

This was our own version of the "Fouga." At Rina's suggestion, we named it "Tsukit" (Swallow).

In 1960, Tzukit, hardly recognizable from the original and far more in keeping with our needs, triumphantly rolled out of the hangar on its inaugural flight. All the ministers, dignitaries, important guests, and of course, Prime Minister David Ben-Gurion attended this memorable event: a jet-propelled fighter plane, built in Israel.

At the height of the ceremony, I came up to Weizman and said, "Please give me your hand." I took his hand and turned it palm upward and asked, "Where is the hair on your palm?" He didn't answer, but knew full well what I was referring to.

This formidable bird, with such a gentle name, proved its capability the instant it tore through the skies at the inaugural flight and right through all the following wars.

We developed personal, as well as business, relations with the private sectors. I became friends with Marcel Dassault, France's premier industrialist, a Jewish man, as we were constantly reminded, whose name originally was Block. He was a survivor of a concentration camp. After the war, he took on the code name of his brother, who was killed in the French resistance. His company, Avions, helped us acquire all we needed in order to create our own planes.

I went to France on business trips frequently, sometimes for several weeks at a time, and learned the French version of business meetings. I would arrive at the office at 10 a.m. and shortly after, the conversation would turn to where we were going to have lunch, what the menu was at that particular restaurant, and the appropriate wine. By then it was noon. After a lengthy, leisurely, and delicious lunch and wine, we began negotiations. If we reached a stalemate, we took a coffee break. Eventually, an amicable agreement was reached, and the papers were signed. Whether or not we had reached the final stage, we all went to dine in some fancy restaurant for dinner. Sometimes it took days to reach the final stage, so the daily routine was followed. I could never tell Rina exactly how long the trip would take. Somehow, eventually, deals were concluded. I explained to Rina why my trips to Paris invariably extended beyond my estimates. She never questioned me.

I took my management team with me whenever it was necessary. We acquired French planes — Mysteres, Vautours, and Oragans — and serviced them. We adapted them all to the needs of the Israeli air force. We shared our technical developments with the French. During those years, we acquired prototypes and parts for the Jericho missiles and gradually learned to produce them on our own.

This amicable relationship lasted for years, even during the 1957 war in which England, France, and Israel combined forces against the Egyptians.

Our relationship with the French was precarious. They respected our skills but didn't like Jews. They didn't like Americans either. As one of them put it to me, "Don't tell them you're Jewish. And don't say you're American. Tell them you're Israelis. We like Israelis." Business was business.

David Ben-Gurion, with his acute intuition, never fully trusted the French. "Why did they surrender to the Nazis?" he questioned.

In 1959, I approved a business deal with foreign companies that were already engaged in aircraft electronics. I foresaw a huge potential in developing an electronics sub-company, not only for aircraft. Not surprisingly, the entire government saw this as an absurd project. Whatever David Ben-Gurion and I suggested was considered infeasible, impractical, and unnecessary by the government, for no apparent reason. They didn't justify their views, just said it's not a good idea. I went ahead with it anyway. We named it ELTA. We started off as a workshop for light industry outside of the IAI premises, in Ashdod. We developed aircraft electronics for IAF and found a market in private companies, such as in pharmaceuticals. ELTA was instrumental in the success of the future wars and confrontations with the enemy. It was the first division that was located outside the IAI grounds.

23

ISRAEL AIRCRAFT INDUSTRIES

Within a year after its inaugural flight, the Tsukit made so much progress that we had the confidence to branch out in other directions. We designed the instruments for an Israeli submarine called the Tanin, or Crocodile.

Another dream I had was to build a business jet. I needed investment partners, and the first person I thought of was Bill Lear, whom I knew casually. I met with him in Geneva and showed him the blueprints. He belittled the blueprints as substandard. Three years later, Lear created the Learjet 23 based on the blueprints and made his fortune. Yet another betrayal.

With all the expansion going on, it was time to restructure the company. It was no longer just a repair and maintenance company. In 1963 we renamed it Israel Aircraft Industries, IAI, and divided it into several divisions. The name Bedek remained as the repair, maintenance, and overhaul division. The test flight department was incorporated into Bedek, and all the test flights were done on airplanes that were serviced by Bedek. Tests on the in-flight refueling systems, modifications, repairs, and servicing of the planes were done by our pilots. Shalom Yoran, born in Poland, a Holocaust survivor who had come to Israel after World War II, became director of Bedek. Moshe Arens — Lithuanian born, raised in Israel from the age of 13, educated in America — was in charge of IAI's new engineering division. "Ziggy" Ariav, also a Holocaust survivor from Poland, became director of production. The chief inspector was American, one chief engineer was English, and the other two chief engineers were German Jews. The top management was as diverse culturally as was the rest of the population in Israel.

Over the years, the Production division produced the first plane built entirely in Israel from scratch: the Arava. The engineering division improved on the engines that we received from abroad, including the French Mirage fighter planes. Hugo Meron was the chief pilot. ELTA developed electronic components for the planes. The navy approached us and asked us to make speedboats for them. We created a company in Ashdod that modified speedboats. The propellers were placed on the rear of the boat, in a way that gave extra power and greatly increased the speed. We modified the Stratacruisers and delved into designing an executive jet plane: the Jet Commander.

Israel Aircraft Industries was becoming recognized as one of the foremost aircraft companies in the world. Our list of clientele grew to include many international companies, each one with their own specific requirements and problems that needed solutions. We sold Arava, Swallows, Ouragans, and Gabriel sea-to-sea missiles.

In 1965, American President Lyndon Johnson offered to pardon us all. I refused to fill out the paperwork. To appeal for pardon? To apologize for what we had done? Absolutely not. Besides, I was too busy keeping IAI competitive in the world market.

I never learned Hebrew, mainly because I didn't have the time to commit myself to it. Some political figures used this to treat me as an outsider. It limited me in a way, but most of my friends and team spoke English, and the highest echelon in the government made sure I understood their opinions, either directly or through interpreters. My children benefited because they were bi-lingual from infancy. I was happy that my close friends Hank Greenspun, Sam Lewis, and Leo Gardner all flew for El Al, and we made sure to have frequent opportunities to socialize.

Occasionally, I managed to take Rina on one of my frequent trips abroad. A truly memorable one was to Cambodia. Prince Yanuk had purchased planes from IAI and invited me to be a guest at his palace. Hugo flew the planes, one by one. When the last plane was ready, I took Rina with us. Stocked up on crackers, salami, and soda water, we were all aboard, ready to cross over Iran, into Pakistan, and then alongside the Himalayas into Cambodia. At some point, Hugo went to the cargo area to fetch more soda. He discovered that in the extreme cold, the soda bottles had exploded; the water had frozen into soda sculptures with metal caps.

In Burma, we found out that Ben-Gurion was at a retreat in a monastery, studying Buddhism. We had dinner with him that evening. After a few days in Cambodia, we were on our way back with a stopover in Iran. The head of the Iranian Air Force, General Khademi himself, met us at the Teheran airport. Iran at that time was one of our most important foreign clients. In keeping with his aim to modernize his country, The Shah of Iran invited the IAI to create something just like it for the Imperial Air Force.

On one occasion, when the director of Bedek, Shalom Yoran, was abroad, I asked him to meet with Mr. Kviatkowsky, a Polish man, member of the board of TWA. TWA had just retired 13 707 Boeing passenger planes, and we felt they could be an asset to IAI. Time was of the essence. The price was so reasonable, a bargain, a Metziya. We couldn't risk these planes being bought up by someone else by the time our government made up its mind. Without consulting the Israeli government, I told Shalom to close the deal. When the ministers in the government heard about this, they were furious. How could this be? What a waste of money. Why does IAI need 13 huge planes like 707s? They denounced the decision, said they had to reconsider the deal, and they held an urgent cabinet meeting. Finally, after hours of deliberation, the government reached a conclusion. They decided to approve the purchase. Exactly at that moment, the planes had just landed at the airport. This created a great deal of negative publicity in the Israeli press, which, like the press anywhere in the world, wanted to create scandals. In the end, this turned out to be one of the best deals IAI made, both commercially and in security matters. These planes served the air force in many missions.

David Ben-Gurion called a meeting with Moshe Dayan and me. In his usual blunt way he asked if we could design missiles.

"That's a tough one. Missiles are complex," I said.

The Old Man, as everyone called him behind his back, asked, "Is this a yes or a no?"

"Well," I said, "if you put it that way, yes we can. Why the hell not?" Ben-Gurion decreed on the spot that Israel needed to build a missile. That set us on yet another path.

In 1966, an Iraqi pilot deserted to Israel in his MiG. IAI experts discovered the weaknesses of this plane, and Israeli pilots were trained to exploit them in combat. In a dogfight, Israeli pilots shot down six Syrian MiGs.

24

THE SIX-DAY WAR

Shortly after General de Gaulle became president of France, relations between Israel and France began to sour.

In May 1967, President Nasser of Egypt felt that they were strong enough to wage another war on Israel and started preparations. Rattling his saber and mobilizing his troops, he announced that there would be a total war against Israel, which will result in the extermination of Zionist existence. He decided to launch another provocation against Israel. He closed off the Strait of Tiran in the Red Sea, cutting off access to Israel's southern seaport Eilat. At the same time, he ordered all UN Security Forces out of Egypt, and began to amass his army along the border with the intention of attacking Israel.

President De Gaulle demanded Israel's promise that there would not be a preemptive strike against Egypt. If Israel made a preemptive strike, De Gaulle threatened to enforce an embargo on the 50 planes that we had purchased and paid for in full. That was his unequivocal ultimatum. And why? Because De Gaulle, the blatant anti-Semite, was going to dictate what we were to do with planes that we had already paid for. He set the condition that we were not to attack first, knowing full well that if we waited until we were attacked, it would be that much harder to win, the casualties would be higher, and the cost of lives much greater.

On June 5, 1967, the Vautours, Ouragans, Mysteres, and Super Mysteres that our mechanics and engineers had worked on and improved, took off. Israeli Air Force planes equipped with advanced electronics and carrying heavy runway-busting bombs strafed the Egyptian runways at 8 a.m., simultaneously destroying the tarmac and all the planes on the ground. 19 airfields and almost 300 planes within three hours. Had they waited another half an hour or so, they could have killed off all the enemy pilots in the planes as well. But Israel's policy of minimizing human casualties, even enemy casualties, dictated that the attack would be carried out while the pilots were having breakfast in the dining hall. Now their entire air force was grounded, unable to take off.

Sirens wailed. The war had begun. Fighting was heavy. Israel was fighting Egypt on the south and Syria on the Golan Heights in the north. But with Israel's aerial dominance, there was no way for the Arabs to win. The Egyptian radio stations were spouting stories about the glorious victories against Israel, that there was now an Egyptian military governor sitting in Tel-Aviv. Every hour, on the hour, the Israeli stations spoke about heavy fighting. At 2 a.m., for the first time, they mentioned the destruction of the Egyptian airfields and planes. I knew about it from the pilots as they returned from their missions.

On the third day of the war, our reconnaissance planes intercepted a phone conversation between President Nasser of Egypt and Prince Hussein of Jordan. The president was coercing the prince to join the war, claiming that this time they would definitely win, and if the Jordanian army would not join the fight under the Egyptian military leadership, they would not be allowed to participate in the spoils of victory. We immediately shared this information with the Israeli Air Force commander. Prince Abdullah conceded to Nassser and joined the war.

All throughout the war, we had to make sure that our commitments to foreign contracts were not delayed or jeopardized. They would be completed as promised.

The Swallows attacked tanks and ground troops; the Stratos dropped para-troopers, tanks, and jeeps from the Syrian Golan Heights, all the way to Egypt, the Sinai desert, the Gulf of Aqaba, Gaza, and the West Bank. As the Egyptian troops retreated across the Sinai Desert, they discarded their arms and uniforms. The Israelis also picked up one of the very sophisticated MiG fighter planes, which the Soviet Union provided to the Egyptians. In Bedek, it was disassembled, and the secrets of its technology were revealed.

The old city of Jerusalem, home of the holiest sites of the Jewish religion, was taken back. Touching the stones of the ancient Western Wall again was an emotionally charged moment for the soldiers.

The Israelis were appalled by what they found in East Jerusalem. During the 19 years of Jordanian occupation of East Jerusalem, Jewish holy sites were desecrated. Headstones from the Jewish cemeteries were used to pave roads. The Jewish quarter was derelict, neglected, and vandalized. The Israeli forces occupied the Golan Heights from Syria, the Sinai desert, and the Gaza Strip from Egypt, and the West Bank of the Jordan River from Jordan. In six days, the war was over.

Again, the world would not allow Israel to claim victory. Preserving Arab pride and dignity was more important. A ceasefire was enforced, a strip of paper that could be torn up whenever the Arabs felt they were ready to attack again. A new political reality was created.

Borders were redrawn. Israel inherited the refugee camps strewn all throughout the West Bank and the Gaza Strip, which had been created by the Jordanians and Egyptians for the Arabs who had left Israel after the country declared independence. In these overcrowded nests of poverty and hatred, vicious anti-Israel propaganda and violence was supported by the United Nations. Ben-Gurion wanted to give back the West Bank to Jordan, the Golan Heights to Syria, and the Gaza Strip to the Egyptians, and hold on to Jerusalem, as all the Jewish holy sites had been so desecrated in Jordanian hands. He foresaw the problems ruling over a hostile population. Israel wasn't geared to be a colonial power. But caught up in the euphoria, the rest of the Israeli government didn't see things his way. They said the

Old Man had become senile. And the Jordanian, Egyptian, and Syrian leaders didn't want that hate-ridden population back anyway.

In 1967, immediately after the Six Day War, we created a helicopter plant near Jerusalem and used an airstrip that had belonged to Jordan. This was essential for the security of Jerusalem.

The Soviet Union immediately began to replenish the Jordanian, Egyptian, and Syrian military equipment and planes that had been destroyed by the Israelis in the war.

International terrorism began for the first time, led by Yassir Arafat. He was a self-appointed leader of the refugees in the west bank and Gaza, whom he called "Palestinians." He himself had been kicked out of Jordan for his terrorist activities. An EL AL plane was attacked in Athens. Israel responded by attacking the Beirut airport. A bus carrying children was exploded. Many more acts of terrorism became the norm.

One day, a visitor appeared in my office: Otto Preminger, a famous film producer. I didn't know who he was. After the tremendous success of his film based on Leon Uris's "The Exodus", he wanted to make a movie about the escapades of another hero: a swashbuckling American macho in his cowboy boots and baseball cap, smuggler of arms, who contributed to the creation of the State of Israel. He wanted to make a movie based on my life. I told him that I had done what I believed was the right thing to do, and now I had to develop and run Israel Aircraft Industry. I was too busy to be involved in a Hollywood movie, and besides, there were many secrets couldn't be revealed. That was during the Cold War. After a five-minute meeting, he left.

25
THE FRENCH EMBARGO CONTINUES

We needed the Mirages we had paid for in France more than ever.

We convinced David Ben-Gurion and other prominent people to talk with De Gaulle, to lift the embargo, to release the planes we had ordered and paid for in full.

But President De Gaulle felt slighted by the Israeli attack on the Arabs despite threat of an embargo on the planes and engines if the Israelis attacked the Arabs first. President De Gaulle was adamant in his refusal. The planes were not to be released.

What betrayal. We asked if we could at least get the blueprints of the engines so that we could work on the on our own and adjust them to our needs.

The directors and engineers in SNECMA and Avions — companies that built components for aircraft, were sympathetic to our needs and would gladly help by giving us the blueprints — but De Gaulle, the president of France, said no. Oh, no! Not again! Another embargo. I thought I was through with clandestine operations, defying the embargo by America before the war of independence. And now this embargo by the French! We couldn't count on France's cooperation anymore. With that, I decided to take matters into my own hands. We had to find ways to do things that couldn't be done.

At the meeting with the directors, who conveyed this decision to us, I could sense that Sulzer's chief engineer, Alfred Frauenknecht was unhappy with the decision. Mr. Frauenknecht said he was personally offended by what the French did to the IIIC crates for Israel. They called it III-C-J, the J for Juif, Reminiscent of the letter J on the armbands that the Jews had to wear during the Holocaust.

Later he made a point of seeking me out privately and offering his apologies. Alfred Frauenknect, chief engineer of the jet fighter aircraft division of Sulzer Brothers of Winterhur was on our side! I invited him to dinner at the Springli Cafe in Zurich.

During dinner, I asked him why the "Juif" had annoyed him so. He termed it "typical French indecency." He was of Swiss-German descent. As a German, he said, at the outset of the war he had been a Nazi sympathizer.

Then he became aware of the atrocities that had been perpetrated by his leader on innocent people. After the war, he became a champion of Israel.

Perhaps in his own small way, he could atone for Germany's treatment of the Jews.

We got down to discussing the purpose of our meeting. We needed copies of the blueprints of the Mirage aircraft engines, all the secret Swiss military documents. For a moment I was suspicious of his calm reaction and asked if he could get the blueprints for us. He said quietly that he could, but expected to be paid for the service, not for himself, but as protection for his wife, should anything go wrong. How shockingly easy that was!

"How much do you have in mind?" I asked.

"$250,000. Half in advance. The rest when we have all the copies."

In total disbelief, I agreed immediately. I had expected a much higher sum and was all prepared to bargain. I didn't originally realize that he'd be supplying thousands of blueprints for all the parts in the engines. He assumed that I had taken all this into consideration. I thanked Mr. Frauenknect. He said, "Call me Alfred." After all, we were partners.

I contacted the head of Mossad, Zvi, who started off by giving me hell for launching upon such an endeavor all by myself. From that moment on, it was pure cooperation. Over the next few months, I flew back and forth between Israel and Switzerland.

A man and a woman posing as an Israeli couple were interested in opening a bakery in Winterhur. I introduced them to Alfred Frauenknecht and went back to Israel.

In a separate operation, an entire assembly line, in crates labeled as oil drilling equipment, were transported by ship to Haifa.

Each week, boxed batches of blueprints were picked up by the bakery truck and delivered to an empty warehouse rented by a Mossad agent, located in a hamlet a few miles from the German border. From there, these boxes were transported to another agent who had become friendly with the German customs officials at the border. The agent transferred the boxes into his own car and drove across the border. Another person drove off with the boxes to a private airfield near Stuttgart, from where a small twin-engine transport plane carried the boxes to Frankfurt. Under diplomatic seal, the boxes went into the cargo hold of an El-Al plane. An armored car awaited the plane at Lod and delivered the boxes to me at IAI. Things went rather smoothly, until the final shipment. Then the unexpected happened. The owners of the warehouse had engaged a local farmer to inspect the premises once a month for any maintenance problems, so our placements had to be carefully coordinated accordingly. For some reason, the delivery of the final batch of blueprints arrived a day or two off. The farmer entered the warehouse, saw a stack of cardboard cartons. Curious, he opened one box and saw documents marked SECRET. He brought several of the blueprints to the warehouse owners, who in turn notified the police. By the time our agent drove up to the warehouse for pickup, the building was surrounded by police. The agent kept driving, out of Switzerland, into Germany; this last consignment never reached us. We still had enough to work with. Our bakery in Winterhur closed down. The couple returned to Israel.

For our friend Alfred, things did not end there. His spy trial was the biggest in Switzerland since World War II. He was sentenced to four and a half years in prison and his $250,000 was confiscated. We supported his wife with $600 each month.

I was persona non-grata in Switzerland. Some five years later, Israel persuaded the Swiss authorities to close the file on me and restore my right to visit Switzerland.

With the help of the French blueprints, IAI created our own vastly improved version of the Mirage. Within a year, the Nesher (Eagle) was flying. It was superior to Mirage and on par with the top planes in the United States and Europe. That encouraged us to design an even more advanced version, which we called Kfir (Lion Cub), a fighter-bomber capable of delivering any weapon, including a nuclear bomb. The Kfir was acquired by numerous countries.

Hinting on the French embargo, the well-known Israeli cartoonist Dosh put it very aptly in a cartoon: the kick in the butt that propelled the little Israeli figure into the age of modern technology.

Upon Alfred's release from prison, I invited him and his wife to Israel, just in time to witness the inaugural flight of the Kfir in the Independence Day air show. I offered him an engineering position at IAI, which he graciously declined. To my regret, we never met again.

The French government also put an embargo on five missile speedboats that Israel had bought for the navy. In a variation on the other clandestine operations, the speedboats that were built for Israel were spirited out of Charbourg by the Israel Navy. The "Charbourg" speedboats, too, were modified to fit our needs. We outfitted them with missiles and satellites. The propellers were placed at the aft of the boats, which gave them incredible speed. These boats were essential in providing security along the shores and at sea.

26
AREVA

In 1968, encouraged by the technological advances in IAI, we decided to develop a twin-engine carrier plane that could accommodate 20 passengers or two tons of cargo. This was to be the first entirely Israeli-built plane. Until then, we had built planes from blueprints or modified them from other planes. We called our plane Arava, meaning desert.

Israel was going through an economic crisis, and it affected IAI as well. But I was reluctant to let people go. If the plans to build our own plane were approved, the company would not be affected by the recession. It would avoid the need to fire employees and stem the emigration of Israeli brain power to countries where the future looked brighter. It took quite a while before we got government approval of the plans for the Arava. With some modifications, the first prototype was built. Professor Moshe Arens, director of Engine Division, believed that the potential market would be North America.

We found that the engine in the French Super Mystere was too heavy and consumed too much oil. We decided to substitute it with the Pratt & Whitney J-79, which powered the Sky Hawk. Both Dessault and Pratt & Whitney assured me that it would never work. We did it anyway. With some manipulation, we managed to cram the bigger engine into the smaller space. There were numerous test flights, pushing the planes beyond the limits.

In one disastrous test flight, the plane went into a spin and crashed, killing the chief test flight pilot. Again, I had to pay a condolence call to the widow at their home in a kibbutz. Stoically, though shocked, she spoke to me kindly. She understood that in such a dangerous profession, accidents do happen. I couldn't help but compare this lady to a similar situation when I had to tell Gerson's wife of the accident in Mexico City. The second pilot made it to safety. We continued developing the plane.

On April 9, 1970, the inaugural flight of the Arava prototype was rolled out of the hangar in a ceremony attended by all the dignitaries of the government.

Prime Minister Golda Meir came to inspect the prototype and was very, very impressed. The chain-smoking woman automatically took out a cigarette and lit it. Though I didn't say a word, I merely glared at her, and she might have seen the horror in my face. A cigarette in the hangar? With all the flammable material around? She understood. She threw the cigarette on the floor and stomped it out with her heel.

The air show of the Arava convinced the IAF commanders that it was necessary to upgrade the entire fleet of Mystere.

We frequently had Friday evenings with Shimon and his wife. While he was doing the dishes in his apron, I brought up an ambition that had been on my mind for a long time. I wanted to build an executive jet, which I believed would be both challenging and lucrative. I felt that IAI was ready and competent enough to take on the challenge.

True to form, as we expected, Moshe Dayan and Itzhak Rabin were against it.

We finally managed to get government approval and started the project. We acquired the blueprints from Rockwell Corporation, the entire production line including jigs and fixtures, and 49 planes for a price that was called "the shrewdest deal in aviation history." It was not nearly as complex as other challenges we had faced. We improved on the original planes to accommodate 10 passengers and called the new jet Westwind.

The prototype of the Arava together with the Westwind 1123, participated in the Paris Air Show in 1971. It was the first time that Israel participated in an important international air show, in the presence of French President Pompidou. He refused to lift the embargo that De Gaulle imposed on us in 1967. He said he was pleased that we were building our own airplanes. The Westwind was sold at considerable profit to a tycoon in Europe.

In 1971, behind the scenes, De Gaulle approved the airlift release of the 50 Mirages that had been under embargo since 1967 after the Six Day War. He finally allowed those planes to leave under secrecy. Dismantled and crated, they were airlifted to IAI aboard USAF transport planes.

Reassembled, they were fitted with the engines that were improved upon from the blueprints that we had spirited out of Switzerland.

In 1972, the American Civil Aeronautics Authority (CAA) granted the license qualifying IAI to build the Arava. Th American recognition of the quality of the Arava propelled the plane into the international market, though this type of plane had already been built in the United States, Europe, and even in South America.

The Arava participated in international air shows in Swaziland, Liberia, and Cameroon and was purchased in Thailand, Ecuador, and other countries. The first Israeli-built plane was a success.

27
OTHER TECHNICAL ADVANCEMENTS

A s IAI continued to grow, we expanded into other directions. IAI's MO was to take what was available and improve on it. Whether it was the ejection seats of Dassault's, refuel pods, missile platform, the Vulture planes, or navigational and electronic systems, IAI could improve it.

Nasser was a full-fledged Soviet client. To counter the balance of power in the Middle East, the Americans loosened their rules regarding military exports to Israel and permitted the sale of McDonnell Douglas Sky Hawk fighters, which could stay in the air day and night because of the C-130 Hercules flying fuel tankers. But they refused to sell Israel the refueling pods, so IAI began to develop our own, successfully. We created inflight refuelers, a system of refueling planes while they were in flight. It connected a second plane that flew overhead and pumped the fuel into the jet fighters. That extended the range and flight time of the fighter planes, especially important in special missions and in combat.

In 1967, we went into partnership with an American company, Turbochrome, which produced a special compound for coating engine blades that detected cracks or thinning in this vital piece of equipment. Cracked engine blades were dangerous, a frequent cause of engine failure and crashes. Instead of regularly changing all the blades on all the engines at regular intervals, we replaced only the blades where cracks or thinning were detected, saving a lot of money and time. This procedure also helped to extend the longevity of the engines and increase safety. The American partnership was headed by Maurice Commanday and was part of our Bedek Division. Maurice became a close personal friend.

We expanded into different ventures. Outside the premises of IAI, Mazlat, a company we created got into developing rockets and missiles. This division created types of missiles specifically needed for the security of Israel.

Mabat was another one of IAI sub-divisions, with plants in Ashdod, Beersheva, and other locations around the country. It began developing anti-aircraft missiles for the navy and electronics. With help from the French in the late 1960s, we had begun developing a program of deterrence that included offensive weapon systems. Peres collaborated with me on every step of the way. We collected scientific and technical information and participated with foreign companies in developing our enterprises that could keep us competitive in the business world.

The Gavriel system provided the navy with much needed radar-guided surface to surface and air to sea missiles for offensive and defense missions. We had very stringent quality control systems. Aviation magazines praised Gavriel as one of the best missile systems in the world.

Barak was a subdivision that developed surface-to-surface missiles protecting vessels from air and sea attacks and low-lying planes. Navies all over the world now use this technology.

Our Nesher was another security system we created from the plans we had of the Mirage. Nesher proved itself the hero of the war.

Thousands of employees worked day and night in Lahav, an Israeli subsidiary of IAI, and in IAI to supply planes to our pilots.

The Stratocruisers were also crucial in the success of the wars. We outfitted them with focal-length long-range surveillance cameras, others with in-flight refueling systems. They could now fly as far away as France without refueling. They had swing doors and were equipped to carry tanks, jeeps, and paratroopers.

The air force needed maritime patrol aircraft to keep an eye on the shoreline. By loading the nose of the Westwind with search and identification radar and other sophisticated electronic reconnaissance and navigation systems, we turned the business jet into a military plane and called it Shahaf (Seagull).

Under our wing was another plant, LAHAV that created another Israeli-made plane, the Lavi, to substitute the Sky Hawk and Phantom. We were focused on developing the Lavi as a multi-functional fighter jet. The project was scrapped. The American government forbade the development of fighter planes in Israel for political reasons. Defense minister Ezer Weizman succumbed to American pressure. He said that it was enough to have F-15's, and there was no need to develop our own jet fighters because it would not be economically worthwhile. We felt we could do it cheaper than buying American planes, but Ezer said that money was not an issue. This, said by the Ezer Weitzman who said hair would grow on the palm of his hand before Bedek could create its own airplane.

We continued developing and improving upon the Lavi, and the Nesher, and later even the Kfir, not only for defense but also for combat. We converted large passenger planes into cargo planes, and used them both in civilian and military flights. They were tremendously effective in our wars. Our pilots tested all the planes that we built, modified, maintained, and serviced for the Israeli Air Force and all the international aircraft companies.

We serviced, repaired, and maintained planes owned by Canada, Burma, Uganda, Guyana, South Africa, Poland, Mexico, Ecuador, Peru, and Turkey. We shared our technical skills with the American Air Force. To better serve our customers, we had offices and crews where needed, in London, Paris, Brussels, Burma, and Uganda. We now had about 29,000 employees and were acclaimed as one of the foremost aircraft companies in the world.

To keep up with the technology of modern warfare, what did we need? We needed drones. We can't rely upon anybody else. In 1974, we began to develop Mazlat drones, small self-flying airplanes without a pilot, for the Israeli Air Force. By 1978, they were being tested in flight. They can stay in the air for 51 hours without being refueled. They were made for reconnaissance from the sky, to direct artillery, and to observe fighting on the battlefield. Mazlat was flown at the Paris air show in 1979, and were bought by many countries, including the United States.

We built one of the most advanced underground wind tunnels in the world. It was officially inaugurated in the beginning of October 1973. McDonald Douglas Aircraft Company signed it, and we used the technological information and developed it further.

When we set up shop in a hangar in 1954, we never envisioned that in three decades, our Israeli aircraft industry would exceed our greatest dreams in its capability to defend Israel, and would be on par with the most developed and sophisticated aircraft industries in the world and still going strong.

28
YOM KIPPUR WAR

What I dreaded most was beginning to happen: politics was seeping into IAI. The media was full of criticism, unfounded accusations and exaggerations, against the way the company was being run, and against me personally. High-ranking officers retiring from the Israeli Air Force were seeking senior positions and options were few. The retiring commanding officer of one of the air force bases was Moti Hod, who had been trained by my friends, the MACHAL pilots after the war of independence. He invited me to lunch and had the audacity to say, bluntly, "I want your job." I told him it was unavailable. He said that his friends, Defense Minister Moshe Dayan and CO of the Air Force Ezer Weizman, were backing him on this. Prime Minister Golda Meir, was no help either. I said to her, "You are an American, and I am an American, and we are both fighting for the same cause." The chain-smoking tough cookie became a pussycat when stared down by Dayan. The workers' union was furious. They stood with a sign in English saying "IAI is AL" and blocked the gate, forbidding entry to Hod. The board of directors was also on my side. But Moti Hod was the prodigy of Ezer Weizman, and he knew that Ezer would back him to become director of Israel Aircraft Industries.

In 1973, on the eve of Yom Kippur, the holiest day in the Jewish calendar, there was an emergency meeting of the ministers, and the entire board of directors of IAI was fired. The government was too consumed in this vitally important matter to hear Mossad warning that the Arabs were amassing armies along the border, planning to attack Israel. Mossad had been warning the government for days, but the members of the cabinet were preoccupied with more pressing matters.

The next morning, the morning of Yom Kippur, I got a call at 6 a.m. The Egyptian and Syrian armies were planning a surprise attack on Israel. I immediately called the heads of all the divisions to notify everybody to go to IAI, which, in times of war, became a military base. I was in my office by 6:15.

The "surprise attack" began at 2 p.m. The Egyptian army crossed the Suez Canal into the Sinai desert. Our impregnable Bar Lev line, our "Maginot Line," a maze of trenches, was breached in a blink.

All army reserve soldiers, taken out of their homes and synagogues, were told to appear in their units, but the soldiers along the borders were not notified. The Syrian army units surprised the Israeli soldiers sleeping in their bunkers on the Golan Heights. The Syrians killed them, chopped off their heads, and played soccer with them — their idea of fun.

Our Nesher, built from the plans that we had of the Mirage, was the hero of the war. Thousands of employees worked day and night in IAI to supply planes to our pilots.

American Secretary of State Henry Kissinger personally negotiated with the American government to help Israel by providing the badly needed military planes and equipment. He shuttled back and forth between Washington and Tel-Aviv, and that's when I first met him. Golda sent a note to Nixon, hinting that the situation was so dire she might be forced to use "all available means to ensure national survival." Nixon understood, and ordered a massive airlift. Within 18 hours, American Phantoms and Sky Hawks landed in Cyprus, where the Israeli pilots took over. Stratocruisers flew in. Tanks and armaments rolled out of their huge bellies. Americans flew in 22,000 tons of equipment. South Africa sent an emergency supply of Mirage parts. The Europeans stayed on the sidelines. That was the turning point in the Yom Kippur war.

One morning, I was invited to an informal breakfast with Kissinger at the American Embassy. I was wondering whether he knew that he had a convicted felon at his table. Jokingly, I mentioned it to a State Department security officer, a friend of mine. He said, "Oh, yes, he is fully aware of your 'crimes.' No way could you sit at the same table with an American cabinet official without him knowing from the Secret Service exactly who you are." Logic says that he was also fully briefed on the 1948 Czech "Zebra" airlift. The security officer said that, knowing Kissinger, if asked, he would probably admit that he admired those Jewish boys.

Bedek was in charge of servicing and repairing the planes as they were damaged. In 8-hour shifts, there was someone at the plant around the clock. Planes were being shot down by the enemy's heat-seeking rockets, and an instant solution had to be found. There was no time to go to the drawing boards to create anti-missile equipment. Heat-seeking missiles shoot for the hottest point in the Skyhawk jet fighter, which is the exhaust pipe of the engine. We attached a long metal pipe to each exhaust pipe, which extended way beyond the body of the plane. The tips of those pipes became the hottest point, away from the plane itself. The rockets knocked down the pipe, and the planes continued on their way. After the war, delegations from abroad came to learn how we dealt with the heat-seeking missile attacks.

The Israeli pilots destroyed over 100 Egyptian, Syrian, and Libyan fighters, some of which were French Mirages.

Israeli 3rd Division pushed the Egyptians out of the Sinai Desert back to the Suez Canal. On his own initiative, Ariel Sharon, who was the commanding officer of the 3rd Division, led his forces across the Suez Canal into Port Said and trapped the Egyptian Third Army. With the intervention of Henry Kissinger, Ariel Sharon signed an agreement with the Egyptians to withdraw the Israeli troops from Port Said and return control of the canal. Again, ceasefire imposed by America and other countries ended the war, which lasted 19 days, until October 25. As in the past, the Egyptians claimed victory. Moshe Dayan resigned. So did Golda Meir. Yitzhak

Rabin and Shimon Peres took over. Very shortly after, Ben-Gurion died. The nation mourned.

Infiltrations, altercations, and terror attacks on civilians continued, whenever the Arabs wanted it. IAI was instrumental in the success of every war and each military operation by keeping the air force planes fit, repaired and maintained. That included the rescue mission of the Israeli hostages in Entebbe, Uganda in 1976, and the destruction of the Iraqi nuclear facility in 1978, two events that have made history. These missions are studied in military schools all over the world.

29
UNLIKELY PARTNERS

Shortly after the Yom Kippur War, a prominent figure in world affairs became involved with Israeli politics: Bruno Kreisky, the Austrian chancellor. The offspring of a Jewish textile tycoon, he was asked by Anwar Sadat, President of Egypt to "halt the state of war between Israel and Egypt." Peres introduced me to Kreisky, and we hit it off. Unpretentious and witty, he won my respect. He offered me a job as his personal adviser on all things related to airplanes. I took the job, and Rina hoped I would finally bring home a sizable paycheck. That didn't quite happen. I commuted between Vienna and IAI, maneuvering both jobs while also trying to drum up work for IAI. The war had drained Israel's finances, so IAI was forced to compete aggressively in the world market. We did it. Within a few years, our reputation escalated globally, and we became a major factor in Israel's economy, as well as its security.

In 1977, the opposition party, Likud, headed by Menahem Begin, won the elections and there was a major shift in Israeli politics. IAI was no longer a priority in the eyes of the government.

Shortly after the election, President Sadat of Egypt came to Israel to sign a pact of non-aggression with Israel. Menahem Begin, who had considered Ben-Gurion's acceptance of the partition plan "not a tactical error, nor a strategic one, but a historical crime," signed the pact. It was not a peace treaty in the real sense, but at least there was quiet on the Egyptian front.

This moment of glory was Sadat's death sentence. Intricate Israeli politics prevented the Israeli-Egyptian peace plans to materialize, and Sadat was murdered by his own people in his own country.

In various periods, we dealt with some very unlikely partners. One of the most colorful characters I met was Idi Amin, President of Uganda, who coveted our planes, but didn't think he had to pay for them. Everybody else was ready to give him everything for free! But IAI did not. He asked me to send pilots and mechanics to Entebbe to train his people in the intricacies of repairing and flying planes. Our experts were there for a couple of years, until the Arab countries and the Palestine Liberation Organization (PLO) — created by Yasser Arafat on the West Bank after the Six Day War — convinced him that it was more lucrative to kick out the Israelis and be friends with the Arabs. Having lived in Entebbe and trained the Ugandans to repair planes, the Israelis were familiar with the layout of airport. So, when hijackers seized an Air France plane bound for Lod airport, with mainly Israelis aboard, our 707 flown by IAI pilots accompanied by three C-130's rescued the hostages in a mission that made aviation history.

Another unlikely partner was the Shah of Iran, who benefited largely from the Israeli-Arab conflict. He felt that siding with the Israelis, who were more technically developed, was more beneficial. He was interested in Israeli military hardware and saw the IAF as a model for an Iranian Airscraft Industry. He wanted to create such a facility in Iran. Our crew was stationed in Teheran, and I flew there frequently. I landed a contract to redesign the airport and establish technical schools and other joint ventures. But that was not to be. When the Shah was deposed in 1977, and Ayatolla Khoumeini stepped in, the dynamics changed. The Israeli contingency was sent home, and the Iranian friendship with Israel ended.

30
RESIGNING FROM IAI

I had to abide by my own decision, as president of IAI, that retirement age should be 65. I realized much later that there was still so much to offer at that stage of my life. I had visions and ideas, and the mental capacity to contribute to further development of IAI. I resigned in 1982.

I couldn't sit still. I had to get involved in something meaningful. I delved into several projects. Some didn't go the way I wanted them to, some didn't pan out at all. None were as challenging and gratifying as the experiences I had helping Israel in its fight for independence and the creation and expansion of Israel Aircraft Industries. I missed having tea after work with my team in the workshops of IAI and getting to know them personally.

I had taken my reputation with me, but only my reputation and not the industrial power and leverage.

I wasn't job hunting, but I was offered high executive positions by Boeing, Lockheed, and GE at exorbitant salaries. Though it was tempting, I turned each offer down. I did not see myself as an employee again, answerable to management. I had put the best part of my life into Israel, and none of these companies had any connection to Israel. None could have benefited Israel.

I had started Bedek in 1953 in a shack with about 150 employees. By the time I resigned from IAI in 1982, there were 29,000 employees. In less than 30 years, the blink of an eye in historical terms, Israel Aircraft Industries had become one of the most advanced companies in the world in aeronautics. Continuing to grow and develop, it is now officially known as Israel Aerospace Industries, creating in-flight refueling systems, fighter planes, and rockets and satellites, out there in outer space along with the big guys. That exceeded my wildest dreams and ambitions.

For a salary of $1 a year, I devoted my full time as consultant to Shimon Perez on matters relating to the government. I served as technical advisor to the Prime Minister, and in that capacity, through the years came into close contact with figures as diverse as Ronald Reagan and Ariel Sharon, CIA Director Robert McFarlane, and Crown Prince Faud of Saudi Arabia, and some nefarious names along the way. I discussed a joint desalinization program with King Hussein of Jordan. I was an unofficial aviation consultant to Austrian Chancellor Bruno Kreisky in Vienna, and in Washington, explained to President Reagan Israel's opposition to the sale of AWACS aircraft to the Saudis. My forays into politics weren't always successful, but one in 1986 was gratifying: the Ethiopian government suddenly allowed its Jews to immigrate to Israel, but the move would entail crossing through Sudan. Since I had previously met President Numeri, I felt comfortable asking him for a business deal. In return for Israeli arms and a training program for the Sudanese soldiers, Numeri would allow us to establish a refugee camp, a sort of "resort," on the Red Sea. From there, through "Operation Moses," some 20,000 Ethiopian Jews were saved from starvation and immigrated to Israel.

I invested in several projects that I found to be significant, some more others. I tried in vain to create separation of religion and state by changing the parliamentary elections system in Israel.

Nothing I did was as challenging and gratifying as working with airplanes. We participated in every aspect of Israel's security, defense, self-sufficiency, and economy. What more could I have dreamed of?

Now that I was retired, I had time to reflect upon chance encounters, the turning points in our lives, about circumstances, momentary events, and spontaneous decisions that change the course of a person's life, other people's lives, or even the course of history. I sometimes wonder what my life would be like if I had not met Fred Levine at a crucial moment. Everything would have been different. How would my personal life have evolved?

I reflect on the lives I changed, the families that were shattered by participating in the cause I was so drawn to, the employees who came to Israel knowing nothing about aircraft and made gratifying careers in Israel Aircraft Industries. Someone we will never meet can alter our path irrevocably, and we can mess up lives and dreams of strangers whom we have never met, without even being aware of it.

I was called a thief, a smuggler, a con man. I wouldn't have needed to resort to all that if there was more compassion in the world. If the country that I loved more than any other, and other countries as well, had not enforced embargoes and helped the most persecuted people in the world when they needed it most, when they were fighting for their very survival, I would gladly have done my share in helping them legally.

What if Ben-Gurion hadn't sought me out in Burbank because he needed me in Israel? What if we hadn't seen the importance of aerial dominance and self-sufficient military defense?

What if Israel had not gotten the planes and weapons that we smuggled in? Would Israel have won the war? Would Israel have survived at all? What would the Israeli Air Force and the Israel Aircraft Industries have been today, or had they even existed, without the planes, tanks, guns, and ammunition that we provided for them? Every tank, machine gun, bullet, airplane, and spare part that we smuggled in, that we were tried and convicted for, deprived of our civil rights for life, was for creating the state of Israel. The people fought bravely. There was no end to their ingenuity and self-sacrifice. Israel couldn't have survived without their dedication. And without ours.

And if Israel had lost any of the wars, how would the annihilation of Israel have affected Jews of the world today?

What if I hadn't realized at the age of 11 that airplanes were my passion?

Do we even know which of our decisions will have repercussions outside of our personal lives?

Would I, could I, have done anything differently?

On my 70th birthday in 1987, Rina's cousin Navah invited over 100 guests to a surprise party. Among them were so many of the people who were involved with me during my time smuggling airplanes: Hank Greenspun, Teddy Kollek, Sam Lewis. All throughout the evening, memories were evoked. Funny ones, poignant ones, hair-raising adventures. And of course, we remembered all our escapades, all those who gave their lives when they took on the challenge of participating in the creation of the state of Israel.

As much as I hated politics, I was directly involved with the Iranian government in procuring the release of the American hostages.

I have always believed in freedom and equality for all. I was fortunate to participate in the creation, survival, growth, and maturity of a nation of oppressed immigrants and witness a nation of pride and power. This is my story, but not only mine. I didn't do it alone. I couldn't have done it without all the wonderful people around me and the life-long friends I made along the way.

In 1998, President Bill Clinton pardoned me on the day he left office after his second term. After 45 years, all my full rights as an American citizen were restored, the basic rights of a democratic society, the right to vote and to hold government jobs. Cynically, I said, "Now I can get a job as a postman." Without my knowledge, Brian Greenspun, the son of one of my dearest and closest friends Hank, personally presented my case to President Clinton, who acknowledged that the pardon was deserved and long overdue. When Rina thanked Clinton for pardoning her husband for the smuggling operation, President Clinton said, "No, I have to thank him."

I never asked for pardon. I believe that I had done the right thing.

That same year I was awarded honorary citizenship of New York City.

Reader, this is my legacy to you: Live your dream. Dream big.

EPILOGUE

Al Schwimmer passed away on June 10, 2011, on his 94th birthday. Very high dignitaries of the Israeli government and his family and friends attended his funeral.

Of his many exploits, many of which remain confidential, Schwimmer will be best remembered for his decision to ignore the strict letter of the law for a greater good. In so doing he became perhaps the single most instrumental force behind the creation of Israel's illustrious air force.

His eulogies were full of acknowledgment of his immeasurable contribution to the State of Israel, to the Israeli Air Force, and the Israel Aircraft Industries. He had received many awards and accolades throughout his life.

Among others:

Swiss-based International Institute of Promotion and Prestige's annual "International Promotion Award." IAI was the first civil aviation enterprise to ever receive the award.

1968 Rothschild Award Prize for industrial achievement, the most prestigious award in Israel, was presented to IAI. Al's friend, his strongest ally in all his projects from the very beginning, BG, would have been proud to see all this.

1968 Haifa Technion Honorary doctorate of science and technology.

1976 Herzl prize for personal contribution to the defense and safety of Israel.

1999 Air Force Foundation, Gold Wing Award for lifelong contribution to the safety and security of Israel.

2003 David Ben-Gurion prize in recognition and appreciation for his contribution to the security and safety of Israel.

ABOUT AL

D avid Ben-Gurion, first Prime Minister of the state of Israel said, "Receiving the Flying Fortress was of major importance, but the greatest gift that came from the United States of America to Israel was Al Schwimmer."

General Moshe Dayan, Commanding Officer of the Israeli Defense Forces, was by no means a fan of Al's; he never believed in his ideas and was originally against creating an independent Israeli aircraft industry, years later said, "With or without me the wars would have been won, but not without Al Schwimmer. With or without me there would have been the State of Israel. But not without Al Schwimmer."

When Al got an honorary doctorate from Technion, Moshe Dayan read out an imaginary conversation with an insect, "Go, insect, to Al Schwimmer and see for yourself how an ant-like enterprise was set afoot with a bulldozer swing. The analogy is obvious."

In the years leading to the war of independence, Al realized that doing what was right and doing what was lawful were not the same. He disregarded an arms embargo imposed upon what was then Palestine and helped prepare the evolving Jewish state to defend itself by gaining aerial dominance. Yet Schwimmer's efforts were seen by the United States as criminal. He became perhaps the single most instrumental force behind the creation of Israel's illustrious Air Force and the Israel Aircraft Industries.

In Greek mythology, the gods took fire away from the people. At great personal risk, Prometheus stole the fire from the gods and gave it back to the people. He was punished for his crime and his eyes were gouged out. But the people had fire.

Al took tremendous risks to provide precious weapons and aerial defense secretly to the beleaguered Jews, outnumbered and threatened with extermination, who could not otherwise have withstood the attacks of five surrounding armies.

His was a crime, and he paid for it. His misdeeds created history. It turned the tide of Israel's War of Independence. It enabled the nascent nation to flourish and to contribute to the world at large.

Al didn't just live through history. He participated in it. He made things happen, the magnitude of which he couldn't have foreseen.

IN GRATITUDE

The creators of this book wish to acknowledge with deep gratitude the personal contribution of each of the individuals listed below and the part they played in Al Schwimmer's fight to create, protect, and develop the State of Israel. Our apologies to all those whom we omitted to include, unknowingly.

Churchill's quote "Never in history have so many owed so much to so few" is applicable here.

Abe Levine – secretly stored crates with engine and airplane parts in his facility

Bill Gerson – multi-engine pilot; AF major; operated his own flying school

Al Raisin – B-17 pilot

Harold Livingston – radio operator

Buddy Rosenman – navigator

Hal Auerbach – navy bomber pilot

Nathan Liff – junk dealer; supplier of military equipment

Sol Fingerman – radio operator

Jim Wilson – LAPSA's chief mechanic

Milton Lowenstein – Jewish Agency executive

Hank Greenspun – ordinance officer; major; owned Las Vegas Sun paper

Leo Gardner – pilot

Steve Schwartz – navigator

Sam Lewis – TWA's only Jewish captain

Ray Salk – top mechanic

Nahum Bernstein – financial expert; lawyer; ran school for secret agents, Haganah members

Swifty Schindler – pilot; director of LAPSA

Norman Moonitz – B-17 commander

Sheldon Eichel – pilot

Larry Raab – A-24 pilot

Coleman Goldstein – pilot

Charlie Winters – the only non-Jewish B-17 pilot; sold surplus B-17

Arnie Ilowitce

Marty Ribakoff – C-46 pilot

Ray Kurtz – B-17 Squadron Commander

Willy Sasnow - master mechanic; flight engineer for TWA

Elynore Rodnick – flight instructor

Nathan Liff – junk dealer for surplus military supplies

Glen King – mechanic

Sam Pomerantz —mechanic

Milton Russell – pilot

Tryg Maseng (Goy) – pilot

Ray Foster – USAAF B-17 pilot

Phil Schild – USAAF B-29 pilot

Ted Applebaum – USAAF troop; carrier C-46 pilot

George Lichter – USAAF training command

Moe Rosenbaum – USAAF pilot

Lou Lenart – fighter pilot served in the Pacific

Chalmers "Slick" Goodlin – pilot

Leo Nomis – fighter pilot

Bob Prescott and the Flying Tigers

Bill Katz – B-17 pilot

All the men put on trial were young, patriotic Americans and idealists who actively participated in creating the State of Israel during its war of independence.

ACKNOWLEDGMENTS

Acknowledgment from Rina:

After my husband, Al Schwimmer, passed away, I decided to bring his story to life.

I had a mountain of material, including Al's memoirs and the memories he shared with me. I collaborated with Varda Yoran to form his words into a story.

Varda and I plowed through the material, selected what we considered would best bring out the character, vision, and values of Al, and set them in the context of the historical events that took place. I agreed to have it written in the first person because it would define him more and capture his personality. Though my English is good, it's not good enough to write a book. Varda's main language is English, and she had already translated her late husband's memoirs into English, structuring and polishing the manuscript along the way. His book was published.

Since she knew Al, I felt we would be a good team.

Acknowledgement from Varda:

I owe a debt of gratitude to Rina Schwimmer, Al's wife, for the material that she provided and the insights into his emotions that she shared in our conversations, without which there could have been no book.

I took the liberty of writing in the first person, because I wanted to convey what I clearly understood through the entire process of writing this book.

In addition to the personal friendship between Rina, Al, my husband Shalom and me, Shalom worked closely with Al for 22 years in Israel Aircraft Industries. So it is an honor for me to be able to write about this incredible giant of a man — what, where, when, how, and why he did all he did.

I never knew the extent of it, nor the deep commitment and dedication within him and the conviction that what he had done was the right thing.

I also thank my friend Joshua Landes for actively partnering with me to have this book published. He admired Al greatly and participated in having his story known.

ABOUT THE AUTHOR

VARDA YORAN, born in China to Jewish parents from Russia, was exposed to a conglomerate of languages and cultures all her life. She lived in China through the Japanese occupation of China, World War II, the Holocaust, the communist regime takeover, and the independence and growth of Israel. She has lived in China, Israel, London, and currently lives in the U.S. These experiences impacted her work as a sculptor.

Varda translated, polished, and edited "The Defiant," the memoirs that her husband had written in Polish about his experiences for seven years during the Holocaust. From the age of 17, he fought actively as a partisan against the Nazis in the forests of Eastern Europe. This book was translated into Hebrew, Chinese, and Russian.

Shalom worked closely with Al Schwimmer for 22 years and a warm friendship developed. The friendship between the Yorans and the Schwimmers continued, even after both Shalom and Al had retired. When Al passed away, Rina asked Varda to write about him using the material and the memories that Rina provided. The book is a tribute to a remarkable person who showed how one person following his dream can change the course of history.

Over the years, we have adopted a number of dogs from rescues and shelters. First there was Bear and after he passed, Ginger and Scout. Now, we have Kira, another rescue. They have brought immense joy and love not just into our lives, but into the lives of all who met them.

We want you to know a portion of the profits of this book will be donated in Bear, Ginger and Scout's memory to local animal shelters, parks, conservation organizations, and other individuals and nonprofit organizations in need of assistance.

*— **Douglas & Sherri Brown**,*
President & Vice-President of Atlantic Publishing